PASSWORD 3

THIRD EDITION

A READING AND VOCABULARY TEXT

Linda Butler

To Clare, with love

Password 3: A Reading and Vocabulary Text
Third Edition

Pearson Education, 221 River Street, Hoboken, NJ 07030

Staff credits: The people who made up the *Password* team, representing editorial,
production, design, and manufacturing, are Pietro Alongi, Claire Bowers, Tracey Cataldo,
Rosa Chapinal, Aerin Csigay, Mindy DePalma, Warren Fischbach, Pam Fishman, Niki Lee,
Fabrizio Luccitti, Amy McCormick, Robert Ruvo, Kristina Skof, and Joseph Vella.

Development Editor: Penny Laporte
Cover image: Lewis Tse Pui Lung / Shutterstock
Text composition: ElectraGraphics, Inc.
Text font: ITC Century Std Book

Library of Congress Cataloging-in-Publication Data
A catalog record for the print edition is available from the Library of Congress.
ISBN-10: 0-13-439937-4   ISBN-13: 978-0-13-439937-9

Printed in the United States of America
1   16

CONTENTS

SCOPE AND SEQUENCE

Unit/Chapter	Developing Reading Skills	Learning Target Vocabulary	Building on the Vocabulary	Using Critical Thinking	Practicing Writing
Unit 1 LET'S EAT					
Chapter 1: *Crazy about Chocolate* page 2	• Guessing word meaning from context • Identifying the topic and main idea of a reading • Scanning • Understanding cause and effect **Tips** • Not stopping for new words • Scanning for proper nouns	*afford, average, dusty, figure out, find, get to, hide, however, melt, offer, professional, researcher, share, suggest, turn into* **Tips** • Understanding what a phrase is • Practicing the challenging words	• Word Grammar: Nouns (singular, plural, common, and proper nouns)	• **Determining** what the text says • **Identifying** key supporting details • **Understanding** and making comparisons • **Supporting** your opinion **Tips** • Introducing critical thinking	• Writing a paragraph about a food **Tips** • Using your knowledge of parts of speech when you write • Reading your work aloud
Chapter 2: *Comfort Food* page 13	• Understanding text features • Scanning for ideas • Using graphs and charts • Identifying the main idea of a paragraph and the whole passage **Tips** • Relying on context when you meet new words • Noticing definitions in a text	*bored, choice, expect, in general, lonely, mention, natural, nearly, opposite, popular, prepare, rather, specific, take part, turn out* **Tips** • Understanding meanings of *text* • Noticing the context of a word	• Word Grammar: Verbs	• **Identifying** key supporting details • **Applying** information from the text to another context • **Drawing** comparisons • **Supporting** your opinion **Tips** • Figuring out what the main idea is • Seeing relationships between data points in graphs and charts	• Writing a paragraph about how you respond to a situation **Tips** • Talking with a classmate as a prewriting strategy
Chapter 3: *The Love Apple* page 23	• Scanning • Understanding cause and effect • Summarizing **Tips** • Reading for main ideas	*available, accept, area, basis, case, change someone's mind, consider, highly, naturally, no doubt, once, root, seed, serve, tax* **Tips** • Identifying the base form of a verb • Understanding *etc.*	• Word Grammar: Adjectives	• **Recognizing** the purpose of a paragraph • **Analyzing** the writer's use of language • **Supporting** your opinion • **Using** your imagination **Tips** • Understanding the purpose of a sentence or paragraph	• Writing a paragraph about a food you feel strongly about **Tips** • Rereading your work after taking a break
Chapter 4: *Slow Food* page 32	• Understanding text features • Scanning • Identifying the main idea of a paragraph and the whole passage **Tips** • Re-reading to understand more • Looking at text features before you read	*attack, boring, culture, danger, disappear, enemy, join, local, member, produce, reach, rush, terrible, variety, weigh* **Tips** • Turning to a dictionary • Learning words in families	• Word Grammar: Adjectives ending in *-ing* and *-ed*	• **Explaining** your analysis • **Presenting** someone else's point of view • **Identifying** problems • **Proposing** solutions **Tips** • Representing a point of view in a role-play	• Choosing a topic and writing a paragraph or a dialogue **Tips** • Using quotation marks when you copy from a text
Unit 1 *Checkpoint* page 42	• Look Back • Reviewing Vocabulary • Expanding Vocabulary: *Word Families* • A Puzzle: *Crossword* • Building Dictionary Skills: *Using Guidewords, Alphabetizing Compound Words, Entry Words with Superscripts*				
Unit 2 LIFE CHANGES					
Chapter 5: *Life is Full of Surprises* page 50	• Identifying topics of paragraphs • Identifying the main idea of a paragraph and the whole passage • Understanding cause and effect **Tips** • Looking for clues to the writer's point of view	*deal with, disappointed, end up, give up, international, interview, manage to, medicine, patience, score, secure, shock, stage, suddenly, support* **Tips** • Understanding phrases with *medicine* • Learning pairs of adjectives (ending in *-ing* and *-ed*)	• Word Grammar: Phrasal verbs	• **Inferring** information about a person • **Analyzing** a remark • **Interpreting** a person's actions • **Citing** evidence from the text **Tips** • Making inferences	• Writing a paragraph about a personal experience **Tips** • Using the verb *end up* in sentences • Reviewing the prompt after you write

Unit/Chapter	Developing Reading Skills	Learning Target Vocabulary	Building on the Vocabulary	Using Critical Thinking	Practicing Writing
Chapter 6: *"It was Love, So Strong and So Real"* page 59	• Stating topics of paragraphs • Reading for details • Reading between the lines **Tips** • Using topics of paragraphs to create a mental map	*alike, although, awful, be about to, challenge, comfortable, difference, discover, face, for one thing, marriage, no longer, responsibility, stare, total* **Tips** • Learning words in word families • Understanding *although* vs. *but*	• Word Grammar: Count Nouns and Noncount Nouns	• **Supporting** your opinion • **Identifying** the pros and cons in a situation • **Explaining** someone else's point of view • **Evaluating** someone's actions **Tips** • Understanding categories	• Writing an opinion paragraph **Tips** • Giving reasons for your opinion
Chapter 7: *To Live as an Artist* page 68	• Understanding text features • Scanning • Making inferences **Tips** • Reading silently	*after all, against the law, a great deal, control, cover, energy, escape, forward, get back to, hardly, lesson, manage, project, role, talent* **Tips** • Understanding *after all*	• Word Grammar: *Hard* and *Hardly*	• **Synthesizing** information from different texts • **Drawing** logical conclusions • **Assessing** the support for a point • **Explaining** your opinion **Tips** • Evaluating the support for an opinion	• Writing a paragraph to describe a person **Tips** • Using *a great deal (of)* • Proving support for your main idea
Chapter 8: *An Amazing Woman* page 77	• Reading for details • Understanding cause and effect • Summarizing **Tips** • Reading between the lines	*amazing, aware, believe in, brave, career, encourage, except, instead, lead, fear, matter, notice, power, value, wise* **Tips** • Using *aware (of)*	• Word Grammar: Some Meanings and Uses of *Value*	• **Evaluating** the support for an idea • **Analyzing** the use of quotations • **Synthesizing** information • **Explaining** the text **Tips** • Summarizing a reading • Understanding the purpose of a quotation	• Writing a response to the reading **Tips** • Writing sentences with *instead (of)* • Writing sentences with *encourage*
Unit 2 *Checkpoint* page 86	• Look Back • Reviewing Vocabulary • Expanding Vocabulary: *Recognizing Parts of Speech* • A Puzzle: *Word Search* • Building Dictionary Skills: *Finding Words in the Dictionary*				
Unit 3 THE OCEAN					
Chapter 9: *What Does the Ocean Mean to Us?* page 96	• Identifying topics of paragraphs • Recognizing and stating main ideas • Using graphic organizers **Tips** • Understanding sentences beginning with *While*	*calm, coast, connect, draw, emotion, gentle, heat, make sense, oxygen, relaxed, storm, supply, surface, wave, while* **Tips** • Using *surface of the ocean* • Using *calm* for people or the sea	• Word Grammar: *Ocean* and *Sea*	• **Analyzing** the text • **Identifying** key supporting details • **Supporting** your opinion • **Citing** evidence from the text **Tips** • Entering information into a graphic organizer	• Writing a paragraph about the ocean **Tips** • Using quotations in your writing
Chapter 10: *The Crab* page 106	• Understanding text features • Reading for details • Definitions • Recognizing main ideas and supporting details **Tips** • Reading subheadings • Looking for definitions in a text	*alive, certain, complain, dirt, entire, environment, fair, go on, have in common, interest, keep on, make up, put up with, sharp, shell, up to* **Tips** • Using *interest* • Using *alive* and similar adjectives	• Word Grammar: *Certain*	• **Understanding** technical terms • **Recognizing** the purpose of text inside parentheses • **Synthesizing** information • **Brainstorming** ideas **Tips** • Noticing the uses of parentheses	• Writing a paragraph about an animal you've researched **Tips** • Writing the title of a book

Unit/Chapter	Developing Reading Skills	Learning Target Vocabulary	Building on the Vocabulary	Using Critical Thinking	Practicing Writing
Chapter 11: *Cleaning Up the Ocean* page 117	• Using graphic organizers • Stating topics of paragraphs • Summarizing **Tips** • Noticing the order information is presented in • Noticing parallelism in bulleted lists	*affect, contain, develop, effort, float, in the first place, make a difference, make sure, mess, planet, pollution, recycle, system, technology, volunteer* **Tips** • Understanding *(the) planet* • Understanding *affect* vs. *effect* • Understanding *make a difference*	• Collocations: *Do* and *Make* + Noun	• **Discovering** the writer's opinion • **Analyzing** the language in a text • **Citing** evidence from the text to support your opinion • **Evaluating** proposals **Tips** • Identifying the writer's point of view	• Writing a paragraph based on personal experience **Tips** • Writing sentences with *in the first place* • Prewriting for summarizing a text • Writing sentences with *make a difference*
Chapter 12: *Underwater Wonderland* page 127	• Identifying topics of paragraphs • Noticing clues to meaning • Reading for details • Stating main ideas **Tips** • Learning from captions	*activity, attach, attract, base, basically, destroy, exactly, in all, national, nature, off, point, situation, space, violent* **Tips** • Understanding *attract* • Understanding *natural* and related words	• Word Grammar: Transitive and Intransitive Verbs	• **Identifying** solutions to a problem • **Distinguishing** fact from opinion • **Supporting** your opinion • **Evaluating** the support for an idea **Tips** • Distinguishing between fact and opinion	• Writing a paragraph about a natural wonder **Tips** • Writing sentences with transitive and intransitive verbs
Unit 3 *Checkpoint* page 137	• Look Back • Reviewing Vocabulary • Expanding Vocabulary: *Uses of adverbs* • A Puzzle: *Crossword* • Building Dictionary Skills: *Interpreting Dictionary Entries*				

Unit 4   IT'S ALL IN YOUR HEAD

Unit/Chapter	Developing Reading Skills	Learning Target Vocabulary	Building on the Vocabulary	Using Critical Thinking	Practicing Writing
Chapter 13: *Food for Thought* page 144	• Scanning • Stating the main ideas of paragraphs and the whole text • Making inferences **Tips** • Recognizing what *Luckily* signals	*according to, advanced, amount, create, effect, feed, immediately, increase, influence, luckily, mean, no matter, or so, powerful, realize, weight* **Tips** • Using *influence* • Understanding *mean*	• Collocations: *Amount*	• **Citing** evidence from a text • **Assessing** a text for missing information • **Inferring** meaning • **Examining** your response to advice from a text **Tips** • Making inferences	• Writing a paragraph about food and the brain **Tips** • Understanding collocations • Writing sentences to introduce your own beliefs
Chapter 14: *Your Memory at Work* page 154	• Identifying topics of paragraphs • Recognizing main ideas of paragraphs and the entire text • Summarizing **Tips** • Appreciating comparisons in the text	*apply, closet, concern, connection, imagine, lecture, look up, memory, notes, region, review, store, term, unfortunately, weak* **Tips** • Recognizing *luckily* and *unfortunately* as antonyms • Using *concern* and *concerning*	• Word Grammar: Meanings and Uses of *Memory*	• **Examining** the writer's opinion • **Applying** information from the text to other situations • **Citing** evidence from a text • **Analyzing** a comparison **Tips** • Inferring the writer's opinion	• Writing a paragraph about memories **Tips** • Using *take* to collocate with *notes* • Writing sentences with *lecture*
Chapter 15: *Sleep and the Brain* page 163	• Understanding text features • Reading for details • Identifying cause-effect relationships • Summarizing	*active, divide, focus, get over, include, nap, pay attention, period, pronounce, rate, schedule, season, series, set, that is* **Tips** • Using *series* • Using prepositions after *focus* and *pay attention* • Understanding *get over*	• Collocations: Verb + Noun Pairs	• **Analyzing** a comparison in the text • **Interpreting** a graph • **Identifying** key supporting details • **Evaluating** advice from a text **Tips** • Using text features to aid comprehension	• Writing a paragraph about sleep **Tips** • Writing sentences with *that is*

Unit/Chapter	Developing Reading Skills	Learning Target Vocabulary	Building on the Vocabulary	Using Critical Thinking	Practicing Writing
Chapter 16: *In Your Dreams* page 174	• Scanning • Distinguishing fact from opinion • Summarizing	*claim, daily, discovery, explanation, in fact, make up one's mind, on the other hand, record, right away, search, somehow, still, useful, whenever, whether*	• Phrases with *Right*	• **Identifying** similarities and differences • **Drawing** logical conclusions • **Summarizing** key details • **Applying** information from a text	• Writing a paragraph about making decisions
	Tips • Recognizing what *On the other hand* signals • Understanding sentences with *In fact*	**Tips** • Understanding *search* • Understanding *vs.*		**Tips** • Applying information from a text to another situation	**Tips** • Writing sentences with indefinite pronouns • Using a prewriting strategy to capture ideas
Unit 4 *Checkpoint* page 183	• Look Back • Reviewing Vocabulary • Expanding Vocabulary: *Word Families* • A Puzzle: *Word Search* • Building Dictionary Skills: *Words with Multiple Meanings*				

Unit 5   COMMUNICATION

Unit/Chapter	Developing Reading Skills	Learning Target Vocabulary	Building on the Vocabulary	Using Critical Thinking	Practicing Writing
Chapter 17: *Who Does It Better?* page 192	• Reading for details • Using graphic organizers • Understanding main ideas and supporting details	*compete, direction, distance, female, ground, invention, invitation, low, male, personal, sense, straight, through, training, voice*	• Meanings and Uses of *Low*	• **Analyzing** a writer's conclusion • **Identifying** key supporting details • **Inferring** meaning from the text • **Applying** concepts from the text	• Writing a paragraph about an animal
	Tips • Focusing on the writer's last words	**Tips** • Understanding phrases with *compete* • Understanding *through* • Using *male* and *female*		**Tips** • Drawing conclusions	**Tips** • Adding a photo to your paragraph
Chapter 18: *When and Why We Laugh* page 201	• Understanding clues to meaning • Determining main ideas • Reading for details	*actually, attractive, behavior, carry out, express, in other words, in spite of, lab, laughter, prefer, smoothly, social, stranger, study, warn*	• Collocations: Verbs + Prepositions	• **Summarizing** key details • **Drawing** logical conclusions • **Interpreting** a speaker's words • **Citing** evidence from a text	• Writing a paragraph about laughter
	Tips • Noticing the functions of first and last paragraphs • Reading a description of a scientific study	**Tips** • Understanding the use of *actually* • Using *express*			**Tips** • Capturing the main idea of a text
Chapter 19: *The Inventor of the Telephone* page 211	• Noticing text organization • Making inferences • Summarizing	*afterward, come down with, deaf, get along without, go wrong, in addition to, in order to, partly, press, separate, shout, speech, various, waste, wire*	• Nouns as Modifiers	• **Inferring** information • **Citing** evidence from a text • **Analyzing** an individual's behavior • **Drawing** conclusions	• Writing a paragraph about an invention
		Tips • Understanding *get along with/without* • Understanding *various* and related words • Using *afterward(s)* or *after that*		**Tips** • Noticing how a text is organized	**Tips** • Writing sentences with *in addition (to)* • Using a concept map as a prewriting tool
Chapter 20: *Speaking with Your Eyes* page 220	• Defining terms • Understanding cause and effect • Distinguishing fact from opinion	*allow, attraction, bring about, chances are, directly, including, in person, maintain, on purpose, polite, refer to, round, sign, space, term*	• Word Grammar: *Allow vs. Let*	• **Drawing** a comparison • **Analyzing** a text • **Hypothesizing** about various situations • **Applying** ideas from the text	• Writing a paragraph about the eyes
	Tips • Rereading first and last paragraphs	**Tips** • Understanding the meanings and uses of *sign*		**Tips** • Understanding pronoun reference	**Tips** • Using quotation marks around a saying
Unit 5 *Checkpoint* page 230	• Look Back • Reviewing Vocabulary • Expanding Vocabulary: *Word Families* • A Puzzle: *Crossword* • Building Dictionary Skills: *Words with Multiple Senses*				

THE THIRD EDITION OF THE *PASSWORD* SERIES

Welcome to the third edition of *Password*, a series designed to help learners of English develop their English-language reading skills and expand their vocabularies. The series offers theme-based units which include:

- engaging nonfiction reading passages,
- a variety of activities to develop reading and critical thinking skills, and
- exercises to help students understand, remember, and use new words and phrases.

Each book in the *Password* series can be used independently of the others, but when used as a series, the books will help students reach the 2,000-word vocabulary level, at which point, research has shown, learners can begin to read unadapted texts.

The *Password* approach to reading skill development for English-language learners is based on the following ideas:

1. The best way for learners to develop their English reading skills is to read English-language materials at an appropriate level.

Attractive, high-interest materials will spark learners' motivation to read, but to sustain that motivation, "second language reading instruction must find ways to avoid continually frustrating the reader."[1] Learners of English need reading materials at an appropriate level of difficulty, materials that do not reduce them to struggling to decipher a puzzle. Materials at an inappropriate level will not allow learners to develop reading strategies but rather will discourage them from reading.

The level of difficulty of ELT materials is determined by many factors, such as the learner's familiarity with the topic, the learner's L1 reading skills, the length and structure of the words, sentences, and paragraphs, and the structure of the text as a whole. These are among the factors that influence the construction of all good ELT reading materials and the way they gradually increase in difficulty. However, an additional, critical factor in determining the difficulty of a text for English language learners is the familiarity of the vocabulary. Note that:

> There is now a large body of studies indicating that poor readers primarily differ from good readers in context-free word recognition, and not in deficiencies in ability to use context to form predictions.[2]

Learners of English must be able to recognize a great many words on sight so that they can absorb, understand, and react to the text much as they would to a text in their first language.

The *Password* series is distinguished by its meticulous control and recycling of vocabulary so that the readings consistently maintain an appropriate level of difficulty. When learners can recognize enough of the words in their reading materials, they can then develop and apply reading skills and strategies. The result is an authentic reading experience, the kind of experience learners need to become proficient readers of English.

2. An intensive reading program is essential to prepare English language learners for the demands of college and careers.

An intensive reading program means students engage in the careful reading of nonfiction texts with the goal of understanding them in detail, under the guidance of the teacher. A well-designed textbook can play a critical role in helping students not only meet that goal but acquire reading skills and strategies they can apply to further reading. Course materials should provide practice with the types of thinking skills that students need, not only to comprehend explicitly stated information but to interpret texts, draw inferences, analyze the language, make comparisons, and cite evidence from the text to support their views. The materials should also facilitate collaboration with classmates throughout the process. When their classroom discussions are stimulating and rewarding, students are motivated to do the assigned readings, and thus get the reading practice they need.

3. An ELT reading textbook should teach the English vocabulary that will be most useful to learners.

Corpus-based research has shown that the 2,000 highest-frequency words in English (as identified in Michael West's classic *General Service List*) account for about 80 percent of the running words in academic texts.[3] The *New General Service List*, with 2,368 high-frequency "word families," goes even further, providing 90 percent coverage of the words in most general English texts.[4] Clearly, the highest-frequency words are highly valuable words for students of English to learn.

The *Password* target word lists are based on analyses of high-frequency word data from multiple sources, including the Longman Corpus Network. Also taught in the series are common collocations and other multiword units, such as phrasal verbs, while a few target words have been chosen for their value in discussing a particular topic. With the

---

[1] Thom Hudson, *Teaching Second Language Reading* (Oxford, UK: Oxford University Press, 2007) 291.
[2] C. Juel, quoted in *Teaching and Researching Reading*, William Grabe and Fredericka Stoller (Harlow, England: Pearson Education, 2002) 73.
[3] I. S. P. Nation, *Learning Vocabulary in Another Language* (Cambridge, England: Cambridge University Press, 2001) 17.
[4] "A New General Service List (1.01)." (n.d.) Retrieved December 15, 2015, from http://www.newgeneralservicelist.org

increasing interest in corpus-based research in recent years, a wealth of information is now available as to which words are the highest-frequency, be it in US and/or British academic contexts, in written English of various types, in spoken English, and so on. Teachers may worry about how to choose from among the various lists, but at the level of the 2,000 highest-frequency words in general use—the level of the *Password* series—the lists are far more alike than they are different.

While becoming a good reader in English involves much more than knowing the meanings of words, there is no doubt that vocabulary knowledge is essential. To learn new words, students need to see and understand them repeatedly and in varied contexts. They must also become skilled at guessing the meaning of new words from context, but they can do this successfully only when they understand the context.

Research by Paul Nation and Liu Na suggests that "for successful guessing [of unknown words] . . . at least 95% of the words in the text must be familiar to the reader."[5] For that reason, the vocabulary in the readings has been carefully controlled so that unknown words should constitute no more than five percent of any reading passage. The words used in each reading are limited to those high-frequency words that the learner is assumed to know, or has studied in previous chapters, plus the new vocabulary being taught. New vocabulary is explained and practiced in exercises and activities, encountered again in later chapters, and reviewed in the Unit Checkpoints and Self-Tests. This emphasis on systematic vocabulary acquisition is a highlight of the series.

The chart below shows the number of words that each *Password* book assumes will be familiar to the learner, and the range of the high-frequency vocabulary targeted in the book.

The five books in the series vary somewhat in organization, to meet the diverse needs of beginning to high-intermediate students, as well as in the increasing complexity of the reading materials and exercises. All five books will help learners make steady progress in developing their reading, critical thinking, and vocabulary skills in English. Please see the Overview in each book for detailed information about that book's organization and contents, including the exciting new features the third edition has to offer.

Linda Butler, creator of the Password *series*

Additional References

Grabe, William. *Reading in a Second Language: Moving from theory to practice.* Cambridge: Cambridge University Press, 2009.

Liu, Dilin. "The Most Frequently Used Spoken American English Idioms: A Corpus Analysis and Its Implications," *TESOL Quarterly 37* (Winter 2003): 4, 671-700.

Nation, I.S.P. *Teaching Vocabulary: Strategies and techniques.* Boston: Heinle, Cengage Learning, 2008.

Schmitt, Norbert, and Cheryl Boyd Zimmerman. "Derivative Word Forms: What Do Learners Know?" *TESOL Quarterly 36* (Summer 2002): 145–171.

Highest-frequency words

Password 1 | Password 2 | Password 3 | Password 4 | Password 5

2,000

Password 5: **target words** *absence, acceptable, advantage,...*

1,500

Password 4: **target words** *appear, attach,...*

Password 5: **words assumed** *a/an, able, about, active, address, adult, agree, almost, amount, appear, attach,...*

1,200

Password 3: **target words** *active, amount,...*

Password 4: **words assumed** *a/an, able, about, active, address, adult, agree, almost, amount,...*

900

Password 2: **target words** *able, adult,...*

Password 3: **words assumed** *a/an, able, about, address, adult, agree, almost,...*

600

Password 1: **target words** *agree, almost,...*

Password 2: **words assumed** *a/an, about, address, agree, almost,...*

300

Password 1: **words assumed** *a/an, about, address,...*

[5] Nation 254

OVERVIEW OF *PASSWORD 3*, THIRD EDITION

Password 3 is intended for students who need to build a solid foundation for reading in English, whether for academic purposes or for their careers. Each of the 20 chapters features an engaging nonfiction reading passage as the basis for a variety of activities to help students develop their reading, critical thinking, speaking, writing, and vocabulary skills.

The book assumes students start out with a vocabulary of about 900 words in English, and it teaches over 300 more of the high-frequency words and phrases that students most need to know. In each chapter, fifteen words and phrases are highlighted in the reading passage and taught in the exercises. All are recycled in readings and exercises in later chapters. Because of the systematic building of vocabulary, as well as the progression of the skills work, it is best to do the chapters in order.

The target vocabulary consists primarily of words found among the 1,200 highest-frequency words in English. Other, lower-frequency words and phrases are targeted for their usefulness in discussing a particular theme, as in the new unit on the ocean, where the words *coast*, *surface*, and *environment* are taught.

Organization of the Book

Password 3 contains five units, each with four chapters and a *Checkpoint* chapter. Vocabulary Self-Tests are found after Units 2, 4, and 5. The answers to the Self-Tests and the Index to the Target Vocabulary are at the end of the book.

THE UNITS   Each unit is based on a theme and includes four chapters, each of which is built around a reading about a real person, situation, phenomenon, or event.
★ **New in this edition:** Each unit opens with a *Think About This* question, designed to activate prior knowledge of the unit theme. It will get students thinking and talking about the topic from the start.

THE CHAPTERS   Each of the four chapters in a unit is organized as follows:

Getting Ready to Read—The chapter opens with a photo and pre-reading tasks. The tasks are often for pair or small-group work. *Getting Ready to Read* improves students' reading comprehension by activating schema. The tasks get them to connect with the topic before they read by raising questions, eliciting what students already know, asking for their opinions, and introducing key vocabulary.
★ **New in this edition:** The new, color photo will spark interest in the topic. The *Learning Outcome* tells students the content objective of the chapter: what

they will be reading, talking, and learning about by working through the chapter. Then, at the start of the Reading section, they will find the new *Read to Find Out* question to give direction to their reading.

Reading—This section begins with the reading passage for the chapter. The passages progress from about 450 to about 600 words over the course of the book. Students should do the reading the first time without stopping to look up or ask about new words. Careful control of the vocabulary in each passage means that students will not get derailed by too many new words and can have the authentic reading experience they need to build their reading skills.

An audio program, with recordings of the readings, is included in the Essential Online Resources. Students may wish to play the audio while they reread the passage, as listening while reading can aid comprehension, retention, and pronunciation.
★ **New in this edition:** The four readings in Unit 3 are entirely new, as are all the other materials in those chapters. All other readings have been updated.

The reading passage is followed by *Quick Comprehension Check*, a brief true/false exercise to help students monitor their general understanding of the text. At this point, students focus only on comprehension of the major points in the reading. Vocabulary study and an in-depth examination of the text will follow.
★ **New in this edition:** Students must locate and cite evidence from the reading to support their answers and to make corrections to the false statements. These are essential skills for academic reading.

Exploring Vocabulary—This section teaches the target vocabulary from the reading. In *Thinking about the Target Vocabulary*, students complete a chart with the target words and phrases from the reading organized according to parts of speech. After they circle those terms that are new to them, students return to the reading to see what they can learn about the words from the context in which they are used. Students can do the vocabulary independently or in pairs, but they will benefit from working on this first as a whole class, with the teacher's guidance.

Using the Target Vocabulary follows, with three exercises to help students understand the meanings of the target words and phrases as they are used in the reading and in other contexts. The exercises can be done in class, by students working individually or in pairs, or for homework. In *Building on the Vocabulary*, students learn more about the parts of speech, collocations, and particular target words or phrases. After working through the exercises in *Exploring Vocabulary*, students can turn to their dictionaries for further information, if needed.

★ **New in this edition:** *Vocabulary Tips* teach vocabulary strategies, new terms, and extra information about the meanings and uses of particular target words and phrases.

Developing Your Reading Skills—In this section are tasks that require students to delve back into the reading. Re-reading is a vital part of the reading process, and the tasks in this section motivate students to do that re-reading and thereby deepen their understanding of the text. The tasks include work on recognizing or stating topics of paragraphs, identifying the main ideas of paragraphs and entire texts, scanning for details and ideas, recognizing cause and effect relationships, distinguishing fact from opinion, and summarizing the reading. Developing these skills is essential preparation for academic reading in English.

★ **New in this edition:** New sections have been added to help students understand text features and use graphic organizers. *Reading Tips* teach reading strategies, offer advice on good reading habits, and raise awareness of text structure.

Critical Thinking—This new section for the third edition adds rigor to the discussion of the reading passages by requiring students to analyze and evaluate what the writer is saying before they offer personal opinions and reactions to the reading. Students are guided to examine the text, make inferences, draw comparisons, determine author purpose, cite evidence--in short, to apply a range of vital thinking skills and demonstrate a thorough understanding of the text. Still included from previous editions are community-building questions, inspired by the readings, that get students to use their imaginations and share their own experiences and ideas.

★ **New in this edition:** Questions for discussion promote the critical thinking skills expected and required for success in college and careers in the 21st century. *Critical Thinking Tips* help students to develop those skills and become more aware of them.

Writing—Part A, *Use the Target Vocabulary*, gives students tasks for using the target vocabulary in writing and has students share their work with a partner. In Part B, *Practice Writing*, students write a paragraph on a topic related to the reading. These writing exercises can be used for brief in-class writing, as prompts for journal entries, or for more formal assignments. Writing in response to reading is a way for students not only to develop writing and vocabulary skills but to deepen understanding of the reading and connections to the unit theme. Sharing their paragraphs helps writers develop awareness of writing for an audience and gives their readers an additional theme-based reading experience.

★ **New in this edition:** *Writing Tips* provide strategies to help students become more successful writers.

UNIT CHECKPOINT   Each unit ends with a Checkpoint chapter, which is designed to help students review and expand on the content of the unit. Students see the vocabulary in new contexts and have the chance to test what they remember and can use. The Checkpoint begins with a *Look Back* section, in which students are asked to recall and reflect on what they learned (*Think About This*) and think about their own response to each of the reading passages (*Remember the Readings*). *Reviewing Vocabulary* gives students another point of interaction with the target vocabulary from the unit, *Expanding Vocabulary* teaches students about word families and word parts, and *A Puzzle* puts target vocabulary into a crossword or word search puzzle. The final section, *Building Dictionary Skills*, provides practice based on excerpts from Longman dictionaries of American English. Knowing how to use a dictionary effectively is an essential skill for the independent language learner.

★ **New in this edition:** A *Learning Outcome* introduces each Checkpoint chapter. The Look Back section provides a valuable follow-up to the students' reading experiences in each unit.

THE VOCABULARY SELF-TESTS   Three multiple-choice vocabulary tests appear in the book, the first covering Units 1 and 2, the second covering Units 3 and 4 , and the third, all five units. The answers are given at the back of the book, as these tests are intended for students' own use so that they can review the target vocabulary and assess their progress.

★ **New in this edition:** The Self-Tests have been updated to include the new target vocabulary.

NEW Essential Online Resources

A new set of resources is available online for *Password 3*. It contains:

- Audio recordings of each reading
- Bonus activities for extra practice in timed reading and study skills
- The Teacher's Manual, containing:
  - The answer key for all exercises in the book, updated for this edition
  - Five unit tests with answers, updated for this edition
  - *Quick Oral Reviews*, sets of prompts to use in class for rapid drills of the target vocabulary for each chapter. These drills can be an important part of the spaced repetition of vocabulary—repeated exposures to newly learned words and phrases at increasing intervals—that helps students remember the vocabulary. The Introduction to the Teacher's Manual contains tips on how to use the prompts.

To the Student

Welcome to *Password 3*! This book will help you read better in English and teach you many new words. I hope you will have fun using it.

REFERENCES, CREDITS, ACKNOWLEDGMENTS, AND ABOUT THE AUTHOR

References

Ackerman, J. "How to Nap," *The Boston Sunday Globe* (June 15, 2008): D10.

Cazeneuve, B. "All Chocolate, No Oompa-Loompas," *The New York Times* (December 22, 2004). Retrieved March 17, 2016, from http://www.nytimes.com/2004/12/22/dining/all-chocolate-no-oompaloompas.html.

Cutler, K. D. "From Wolf Peach to Outer Space— Tomato History & Lore," Brooklyn Botanic Garden. Retrieved June 11, 2009, from http://www.bbg.org/gar2/topics/kitchen/handbooks/tomatoes/1.html/.

Milius, S. "Don't look now, but is that dog laughing?" *Science News* 28 July 2001: 55. Science in Context. Web. 9 Feb.2016

Nabhan, G. P. *Coming Home to Eat.* New York: W. W. Norton & Co., Inc., 2002.

Provine, R. *Laughter: A scientific investigation.* New York: Penguin Books, 2000.

Rock, A. *The Mind at Night.* New York: Basic Books, 2004.

Slow Food. http://www.slowfood.com.

Photo Credits

Page 1: Dragon Images/Shutterstock; **2:** Randy Duchaine/Alamy Stock Photo; **13:** SolStock/iStock/Getty Images; **23:** Lidante/Shutterstock; **32:** Edward Bock/Alamy Stock Photo; **33:** Jan Greune/LOOK Die Bildagentur der Fotografen GmbH/Alamy Stock Photo; **42:** Dragon Images/Shutterstock; **49:** Bikeriderlondon/Shutterstock; **50:** Courtesy of Mahmoud Arani; **59:** Courtesy of Arunaa Franklin; **68:** Peteri/Shutterstock; **77:** Edward Stapel/AP Images; **86:** Bikeriderlondon/Shutterstock; **95:** Lee Prince/Shutterstock; **96:** Sborisov/Fotolia; **106:** Xu Yanyan/Xinhua/Alamy Stock Photo; **107:** Pakhnyushchyy/Fotolia; **117:** The Ocean Cleanup; **118:** EPA European pressphoto agency b.v./Alamy Stock Photo; **127:** Irochka/Fotolia; **137:** Lee Prince/Shutterstock; **143:** Sebastian Kaulitzki/Fotolia; **144:** Michaeljung/Fotolia; **154:** Tom Wang/Fotolia; **163:** Voisin/Phanie/Alamy Stock Photo; **174:** Marka/Alamy Stock Photo; **175:** ZUMA Press, Inc./Alamy Stock Photo; **183:** Sebastian Kaulitzki/Fotolia; **191:** Ljupco Smokovski/Fotolia; **192:** Vladyslav Danilin/Fotolia; **193:** Subrata Chakraborty/123RF; **201:** Antonioguillem/Fotolia; **211:** North Wind Picture Archives/Alamy Stock Photo; **220:** Courtesy of Linda Butler; **230:** Ljupco Smokovski/Fotolia

Text Credits

Nightline: Jacques Torres, from ABCNEWS.com.

Acknowledgments

First of all, I would like to thank the people who shared their stories with me so that I could share them with readers of this book: Mahmoud Arani, Vitek Kruta, and Arunaa and Hervé Phalippou. I would also like to thank my students at Holyoke Community College (Holyoke, MA, USA) for their feedback on reading passages, in particular Julissa Garib and Lisandra Zeno, who also let me include excerpts from their journals. Many thanks as well to Rubaba Matin and other colleagues at HCC whose comments on earlier editions of the book were much appreciated. *Un abbraccio* to my brilliant development editor, Penny Laporte.

I also very much appreciate the work of the following reviewers: Simon Weedon, NOVA ICI Oita School, Japan; Joe Walther, Sookmyung Women's University, Korea; Kevin Knight, Kanda University of International Studies, Japan; Guy Elders, Turkey; Wendy Allison, Seminole Community College, Florida; Kimberly Bayer-Olthoff, Hunter College, New York; Ruth Ann Weinstein, J. E. Burke High School, Massachusetts; Vincent LoSchiavo, P.S. 163, New York; Kelly Roberts-Weibel, Edmunds Community College, Washington; Lisa Cook, Laney College, California; Thomas Leverett, Southern Illinois University, Illinois; Angela Parrino, Hunter College, New York; Adele Camus, George Mason University, Virginia, Lynn Bonesteel, Boston University, Boston, MA.

Finally, it has been a pleasure working with Pearson English, and for all their efforts on behalf of this book and the entire *Password* series, I would like to thank everyone on the Pearson English team.

About the Author

Linda Butler began her English language teaching career in Italy in 1979. She earned a master's in TESOL at Boston University and has since taught in several college ESL programs in the United States. She writes and edits online and print materials for learning, teaching, and testing English, and she is the author of many ESL/EFL textbooks, including Books 1 through 4 of the *Password* series and *Longman Academic Writing Series 1: Sentences to Paragraphs.*

UNIT 1
LET'S EAT!

THINK ABOUT THIS

How do you choose the food you eat?

Check ✔ your answers, and add ideas of your own.

- [ ] It tastes good.
- [ ] It's good for me.
- [ ] It's easy to make.
- [ ] Someone makes it for me.
- [ ] Your ideas: _____

CHAPTER 1

Crazy about Chocolate

Chef Jacques Torres

LEARNING OUTCOME

❯ Learn about someone who makes chocolate

GETTING READY TO READ

Talk about these questions with a partner.

1. Which of these do you like? Check ☑ your answers. Then ask your partner.

	You	Your Partner
a. chocolates[1]	☐	☐
b. chocolate bars[2]	☐	☐
c. hot chocolate	☐	☐
d. other foods with chocolate, for example: _____		

[1] *a box of chocolates*

[2] *a bar of chocolate*

2. Do you think chocolate is good for you? Tell why or why not.
3. If you are crazy about someone or something, you like that person or thing very, very much. What or who are you crazy about?

READING

Read to Find Out: What does Jacques Torres say about chocolate?

Look at the picture, words, and definitions next to the reading. Then read without stopping. Don't worry about new words. Don't stop to use a dictionary. Just keep reading.

Crazy about Chocolate

1   How do you feel about chocolate? If you like it, you are far from alone. The question is, why are so many people so crazy about it?

2   Jacques Torres has always loved chocolate. When he was a child in France, his family could not **afford** to buy it very often. They used to have chocolates only once a year, at Christmas. Jacques remembers how he used to take some and go **hide** under the table, with the tablecloth[1] all around him. He didn't want his mother to see how many chocolates he was eating. He says that when he bit into one of his favorites, "That was *heaven!*"[2]

3   When he grew up, Jacques became a **professional** chef. For years, he worked at famous restaurants in France and the United States. Then he left restaurant work to start his own business. Today, he owns nine chocolate shops in New York City, one with a chocolate factory next door. It feels to him like a dream come true.

4   "Everybody loves chocolate," says Jacques, "but it's such a mystery[3] to them. How does this magic happen?" At the factory, visitors **get to** watch how it happens through eleven-foot-tall windows. Jacques **offers** visitors the chance to see how **dusty** brown cocoa beans[4] are **turned into** beautiful chocolates.

5   It's clear that many people **share** Jacques' love of chocolate. His shops sell millions of dollars worth of chocolate each year. **However**, no one thinks of New York City as the world capital of chocolate. That would be Switzerland, a country rich in chocolate factories. The **average** person there eats about 22 pounds of chocolate a year. Next in line after the Swiss are the chocolate-loving British. There are chocolate lovers across all of Europe, North and South America, and Australia, too. Now chocolate makers are looking to Asia for new customers, especially India and China.

6   Why do people love chocolate so much? Many **researchers** have asked this question, and they have studied what chocolate does to the human brain. Scientists have **found** that chocolate has more than 300 different chemicals[5] in it. Which ones give us the good feelings we get when chocolate **melts** in the mouth? That has been difficult to **figure out**.

[1] a tablecloth

[2] *heaven* = a place of perfect happiness

[3] *mystery* = something that is difficult to explain or understand

[4] *cocoa beans* = beans from the cacao tree, used to make chocolate

[5] *chemical* = a substance, especially one made by or used in chemistry

7　We do now know that chocolate can be good for you, especially dark chocolate. So, if you wish, you can say that you eat it for your health. Jacques Torres **suggests** a different way to think about chocolate. "You know, chocolate is like romance,"[6] he says. "It makes your eyes close, your mouth water. It makes you playful." That seems a fine reason to enjoy a little chocolate.

[6] *romance* = the feeling of excitement connected with love between two people

Quick Comprehension Check

A. Read these sentences **about the reading**. Circle T (true) or F (false). On the line, write the number of the paragraph with the answer.

1. The writer says that many people are crazy about chocolate.　Ⓣ　F　__1__

2. Jacques Torres is a French chef and a lover of chocolate.　T　F　____

3. Jacques thinks most people understand how chocolate is made.　T　F　____

4. New Yorkers eat more chocolate than anyone else.　T　F　____

5. Chocolate does something to your brain when you eat it.　T　F　____

6. Jacques wants people to eat chocolate for their health.　T　F　____

B. Work with your class. Share your answers from part A. Go back to the reading to find the reason why a statement is true or false. Correct the false statements.

EXPLORING VOCABULARY

Thinking about the Target Vocabulary

Guessing Meaning from Context

We use words in a **context**. The context of a word means the words and sentences before and after the word. When you read, the context can help you guess a word's meaning. For example, look at the context of *hide*:

> Jacques remembers how he used to take some and go **hide** under the table, with the tablecloth all around him. He did not want his mother to see how many chocolates he was eating.

The context of *hide* tells you that the word means "stay in a place where no one can see or find you."

A. Look at the chart with the target vocabulary for this chapter.

- The left column gives the number of the paragraph in the reading where you can find the target word or phrase. The symbol ¶ means "paragraph."

- Other columns show important parts of speech. The **Nouns** column shows the singular form of any plural noun from the reading. The **Verbs** column shows the base form, or simple form, of each verb.

> **Vocabulary Tip:** A **phrase** is a group of two or more words that work together in a sentence. *Thank you, in back of,* and *for example* are phrases.

B. Which target words are new to you? Circle them in the chart. Then find them in the reading. Look at the context. Can you guess the meaning?

¶	Nouns	Verbs	Adjectives	Other
2		afford		
		hide		
3			professional	
4		get to		
		offer		
			dusty	
		turn into		
5		share		
				however
			average	
6	researcher			
		find		
		melt		
		figure out		
7		suggest		

Using the Target Vocabulary

A. These sentences are **about the reading**. Complete them with the words and phrases in the b ox.

✓afford	dusty	~~found~~	however	share
average	figure out	get to	professional	turns them into

1. Jacques Torres's family did not have enough money to buy chocolates very often. They could not _____*afford*_____ them.

2. Jacques chose cooking and baking as his life's work. He is a _____ chef.

3. Some people are lucky: They have the chance to watch chocolates being made at Jacques' factory. Those people _____ watch it happen.

4. The cocoa beans that Jacques uses have a dry powder on them. It is like the powder on a piece of chalk, or like the very small pieces of dirt in a house. The cocoa beans look _____.

5. Jacques takes cocoa beans, sugar, and other things and changes them into fine chocolates. He _____ chocolates.

6. Many people feel the same way about chocolate that Jacques does. They _____ his love of chocolate.

7. People buy a lot of chocolate in New York. _____, Switzerland, not New York, is the "world capital of chocolate."

8. Some Swiss eat a lot of chocolate every day. Others never eat it. The _____ person is somewhere in the middle.

9. Scientists have learned about chocolate by doing tests and other research. They have _____ that there are more than 300 chemicals in it.

10. It has not been easy for scientists to answer all their questions about chocolate. They have not been able to _____ why it makes people feel good.

B. These sentences use the target words and phrases **in new contexts**. Complete them with the words and phrases in the box.

afford	dusty	found	however	share
average	figure out	get to	professional	turning it into

1. I'd like to take a nice vacation, but I can't _____ to.

2. I need to clean under the bed. It's very _____ under there.

3. Researchers have _____ that the average Swiss eats about 22 pounds of chocolate a year.

4. Jan can afford to buy a car. _____, she can't afford a new one, only a used one.

5. I'm glad tomorrow is a holiday because I'll _____ sleep late in the morning.

6. They are taking that old factory and _____ an office building.

7. We have a map, so we can _____ how to get there.

8. They'll have lots to talk to each other about. They _____ a strong interest in sports.

9. On an _____ day, the doctor sees about 20 patients.

10. Tom dreamed of becoming a _____ soccer player. He thought that would be the perfect job.

C. Read each definition and look at the paragraph number. Look back at the reading on pages 3 and 4 and find the **boldfaced** word to match the definition. Write the word on the line.

Definition	Paragraph	Target Word
1. go or stay in a place where no one can see or find you	2	*hide*
2. makes it possible for someone to have something they want	4	
3. people who study a subject to find new facts	6	
4. changes from a solid to a liquid (like ice to water) because of heat	6	
5. gives someone an idea about what to do	7	

Building on the Vocabulary

Word Grammar: Nouns

Nouns are words for:

people	*student, Eliza, boy*
places	*airport, Mexico, home*
things	*book, apple, the Eiffel Tower*
ideas	*education, hope, information*

Some nouns are written as two words (*hot dog, New York*). Most nouns can be **singular** (only one: *a friend, the door*) or **plural** (more than one: *two friends, the doors*).

A **proper noun** starts with a capital letter and names one special person (*Jacques*), place (*the Pacific Ocean*), or thing (*the Great Wall*).

Most nouns are **common nouns** and do not start with a capital letter (*man, ocean, wall*).

There are two nouns in each sentence. Circle the nouns.

1. They are going to Madrid by train.

2. The researchers at the hospital will figure it out.

3. Cats and dust make me sneeze. Ah *CHOO!*

4. The children are hiding behind the tree.

5. You and Tom can share the cookies.

6. The chocolate melted in my hand.

7. What is Dr. King's profession?

8. I suggest we take a trip to the beach.

> **Writing Tip:** Knowing what part of speech a word is—noun, verb, or adjective, for example—will help you understand how to use it in a sentence.

DEVELOPING YOUR READING SKILLS

The Topic and the Main Idea

Identifying the Topic and the Main Idea

A reading has a **topic**. Ask, "What is the reading about?" The answer is the topic.

A reading has a **main idea**. Ask, "What does the reading say about the topic?" The answer is the main idea.

Answer the questions.

1. What is the topic of the reading? Check ☑ your answer.
   - ☐ a. crazy people
   - ☐ b. chocolate lovers
   - ☐ c. reasons you should eat chocolate

2. What is the main idea of the reading? Check ☑ your answer.
   - ☐ a. Chocolate goes to the brain and makes people do crazy things.
   - ☐ b. Chef Jacques Torres shares a love of chocolate with people all over the world.
   - ☐ c. People eat chocolate because it is a health food that makes us feel good.

Scanning

Scanning for Information

Sometimes you need to find a piece of information in a reading. To do this, you **scan** the reading. *Scan* means to look through the text very quickly to find the information you need.

Read these statements about "Crazy about Chocolate." Scan the reading for the information you need to complete them.

> **Reading Tip:**
> Scanning a reading is a good way to find numbers or proper nouns quickly.

1. Jacques Torres grew up in _____.

2. He grew up to be a professional _____.

3. Now he owns _____ chocolate shops in _____.

4. Visitors to his _____ can watch chocolates being made.

5. His shops sell _____ a year.

6. _____ is the world capital of chocolate.

7. The average Swiss eats _____ of chocolate a year.

8. After the Swiss, the people who eat the most chocolate are _____.

9. There are _____ different chemicals in chocolate.

10. Researchers have studied what the chemicals in chocolate do to

    the human _____.

Understanding Cause and Effect

Sentences with *Because*

Sentences with *because* explain cause-and-effect relationships.

- *Cause* means the reason something happens: *No one knows the cause of the accident.*
- *Effect* means a change that happens because of an action or event: *They studied the effects of chocolate on the brain.*

Sentences with *because* answer the question *Why?* The sentences have two parts, or clauses. The part that starts with *because* can come first or second in the sentence.

*Jacques didn't eat chocolates often **because his family couldn't afford them**.*

***Because his family couldn't afford chocolates**, Jacques didn't eat them often.*

A. Complete the sentences. Find the causes in the reading.

1. Jacques hid under the table because _____

   _____.

2. Jacques left restaurant work because _____

   _____.

3. Switzerland is called "the world capital of chocolate" because _____

   _____.

4. Researchers have studied chocolate because _____

   _____.

B. Circle *would* or *wouldn't*. Complete the sentence.

I (would / wouldn't) like to own a chocolate factory because _____

_____.

CRITICAL THINKING

Discussion

Critical Thinking Tip: In this book, you will be able to practice critical thinking. Using critical thinking will help you read with more understanding.

Talk about these questions with the whole class.

1. Paragraph 2 is about Jacques Torres as a child. Which statement gives the main idea of this paragraph?

   a. Jacques' mother was careful not to let him eat too much chocolate.

   b. Even as a child, Jacques understood it was not healthy to eat a lot of chocolate.

   c. When Jacques was a child, eating chocolate was a special event.

   What information in the paragraph helped you choose your answer?

2. What does the reading say about the Swiss? How do people in your country compare with the Swiss when it comes to eating chocolate?

3. The reading says that scientists have studied chocolate. How would a scientist answer the question, "Why are so many people so crazy about it?"

4. What do we still not know about chocolate? What would you like to know? How would Jacques answer the question of why people love chocolate? Underline the information in the reading that helps you answer this question. Do you agree with what he says about chocolate? Explain your answer.

5. Writing about Jacques in paragraph 3, the writer says, "It feels to him like a dream come true." What is "it"? In what way is "it" like a dream? How did Jacques make his dream come true? What does it take for anyone to make a dream come true?

WRITING

A. Use the Target Vocabulary: Choose five target words or phrases from the list on page 5. On a piece of paper, use each word or phrase in a sentence and underline it. Find a partner and read each other's sentences.

Examples:

I always wanted a pet when I was growing up, but I never <u>got to</u> have one.
The library is a good place to study. <u>However</u>, it closes too early.
I have <u>found</u> that it is not a good idea to lend money to my roommate.

Vocabulary Tip: Do not choose the easiest words and phrases to practice. Writing sentences is a chance to learn more about the words you do not understand well.

B. Practice Writing: Choose one of these topics and write a short paragraph about it. Then find a partner and read each other's paragraphs.

Writing Tip: Read your paragraph out loud to yourself before you show it to a reader. It can help you make sure your paragraph will be clear to your reader.

1. Write about a food that you think is good for people's health. (What is it good for? Who says that it is good? Do you eat it?)

   You can begin: . . . *is/are good for people's health.*

2. Describe a food from your country that many people enjoy. (What is it like? Do you eat it often or only at special times?)

   You can begin: *I come from . . . , and many people in my country love . . . .*

Example:

> ### Apples
>
> Apples are good for people's health. My mother always said, "A diario una manzana es cosa sana." It is the same idea as "An apple a day keeps the doctor away." Most kinds of fruit are good for you. They have vitamins and other things I don't know about, but I know they are good for you. I eat an apple a day and other kinds of fruit, too.

CHAPTER 2

Comfort Food

One woman's comfort food

LEARNING OUTCOME

❯ Learn what *comfort food* means to different people

GETTING READY TO READ

Answer the questions. Then talk about your answers in a small group.

1. Imagine that it is late at night. You have to study, but you are hungry. What would you choose to eat? Name three things.

   _____   _____   _____

2. Do you think these statements are true or false? Circle your answers.

   a. People eat when they are tired.   True   False
   b. People eat when they feel sad.   True   False
   c. People eat when they feel nervous.   True   False
   d. People eat when they want to celebrate.   True   False

READING

Read to Find Out: How is comfort food different for different people?

Look at the pictures, words, and definitions next to the reading. Then read without stopping. Don't worry about new words. Don't stop to use a dictionary. Just keep reading.

Comfort Food

1   It's **natural** for people to eat when they're hungry, but people eat for other reasons, too. Do you ever eat because you're with friends and everyone else is eating? Do you ever eat because you feel tired, or because you're under stress? Many people do. Maybe they have too much to do, or they're having problems in a relationship. So they eat to feel better. But they don't eat just anything. They want a **specific** kind of food. They want food that helps them relax. They want comfort food.

2   What is comfort food? For most people, it's food that is easy to **prepare** and easy to eat. Eating it gives them a warm feeling. It's often a type of food that they loved as children. Maybe they used to eat it at specific times or places. Maybe it's food their mother or father used to make. Comfort food makes people feel, "Somebody's taking care of me."

3   Researchers at the University of Illinois did a survey[1] on comfort food in the United States. They asked over 1,000 people about it. They wanted to know two things: What comfort foods did people want, and when did they want them? The results of the survey were **rather** surprising.

4   The researchers **expected** people's favorite comfort food to be soft and warm, like, for example, the most **popular** comfort foods in Japan, miso soup and soba noodles.[2] But the number one U.S. comfort food was *not* soft or warm. It **turned out** to be potato chips. Another favorite was ice cream, especially among people ages 18 to 34. Not all comfort foods are snack foods,[3] however. **Nearly** half of the comfort foods that people described were healthy, homemade foods, like chicken soup and mashed potatoes.[4]

5   The survey showed that people of different ages want different comfort foods. It also showed that men and women make different **choices**. **In general**, women choose sweet comfort foods. Those who **took part in** the survey **mentioned** ice cream most often (74% of them put it on their list), then chocolate (69%), and cookies (66%). Ice cream was very popular with the men, too: 77% of the men in the survey mentioned it. However, men do not choose sweet foods as often as women do. Men often want hot and salty comfort foods such as soup (73%) and pizza or pasta (72%).

[1] *survey* = a set of questions you ask a large group of people to learn their opinions

[2] *Soba noodles are made from buckwheat.*

[3] *snack foods* = kinds of food that people buy ready-made to eat between meals

[4] *mashed potatoes*

6   The researchers also figured out *when* the people in the study wanted comfort food most. You may think that comfort food is usually for times of stress, or when someone feels **bored** or **lonely**. However, the researchers say that the **opposite** is true. Yes, people do eat to feel better, but more often, they eat comfort foods when they already feel happy. They eat them to celebrate or to reward themselves.[5]

[5] *reward themselves* = give themselves something nice because they did a good thing

Quick Comprehension Check

A. Read these sentences **about the reading**. Circle T (true) or F (false). On the line, write the number of the paragraph with the answer.

1. People eat for many different reasons.   T   F   ____

2. Comfort food is food that makes you feel good.   T   F   ____

3. The researchers studied comfort foods around the world.   T   F   ____

4. Men and women agree about the best comfort foods.   T   F   ____

5. People want comfort food most when they feel sad.   T   F   ____

6. The top comfort food in the United States is potato chips.   T   F   ____

B. Work with your class. Share your answers from part A. Go back to the reading to find the reason why a sentence is true or false. Correct the false sentences.

EXPLORING VOCABULARY

Thinking about the Target Vocabulary

A. Look at the chart with the target vocabulary from "Comfort Food." Two nouns are missing. Scan the reading to find the two nouns in **bold**. Add them to the correct places in the chart. Write the singular form of any plural noun.

¶	Nouns	Verbs	Adjectives	Other
1			natural	
			specific	
2		prepare		
3				rather
4		expect		

¶	Nouns	Verbs	Adjectives	Other
			popular	
		turn out		
				nearly
5				
				in general
				take part in
		mention		
6			bored	
			lonely	

B. Which words and phrases are new to you? Circle them in the chart. Then find them in the reading. Look at the context. Can you guess the meaning?

Using the Target Vocabulary

A. These sentences are **about the reading**. What is the meaning of each **boldfaced** word? Circle a, b, or c.

1. People eat when they are hungry. That's the **natural** thing to do. In this sentence, *natural* means

   a. crazy, stupid.   **(b.)** normal, usual.   **c.** strange, surprising.

2. Sometimes we get hungry for a **specific** kind of food—comfort food. A specific kind is

   a. one kind and no other.   **b.** any kind we can get.   **c.** every kind there is.

3. Comfort food doesn't usually take a lot of work. It's easy to **prepare**. *Prepare* means

   a. melt.   **b.** turn into.   **c.** get ready.

4. The information from the survey was **rather** surprising. *Rather* means

   a. more than a little.   **b.** not at all.   **c.** of course.

5. The researchers **expected** the top comfort food to be warm and soft. When you expect something, you

   a. can afford it.   **b.** think it will happen.   **c.** share it.

6. Many of the comfort foods people talked about were snack foods, but **nearly** half of the foods were not. *Nearly* means

   a. completely.   **b.** almost.   **c.** ever.

7. Men and women often make different **choices** in comfort food. Their choices are the things that they
   - **a.** figure out.
   - **b.** throw.
   - **c.** decide on.

8. Many women in the survey **mentioned** ice cream. If you mention something, you
   - **a.** say a few words about it.
   - **b.** get to do it.
   - **c.** do research on it.

9. Some people eat comfort food when they are **lonely**. It makes them feel less alone. Lonely means
   - **a.** tired of being with people.
   - **b.** away from friends and feeling sad.
   - **c.** happy and relaxed.

10. Some people eat when they feel **bored**. It gives them something to do. Bored means
   - **a.** tired of having nothing fun to do.
   - **b.** very busy.
   - **c.** ready to go to work.

B. These sentences use the target words **in new contexts**. Complete them with the words in the box.

bored	expect	mention	nearly	rather
choice	lonely	natural	prepared	specific

1. They _____ a wonderful dinner for their guests.

2. Jane talked about the book she's reading, but she didn't

   _____ the name of it.

3. The students almost went to sleep in class. They were very

   _____.

4. Let's call Dave and see if he's OK. He has no family, and I think he gets

   _____ on holidays.

5. Which movie would you like to see? My first _____ would be

   that new action movie.

6. This is Miki's first trip away from home. It's _____ that she

   misses her family.

7. The party was a complete surprise to Dan. He didn't _____

   it.

8. I don't have any _____ plans for the weekend. I just want to relax.

9. This box is _____ heavy. Can you help me with it?

10. The potatoes need to cook for just a few more minutes. They're

_____ done.

C. Read the sentences. Guess the meaning of the **boldfaced** target words and phrases from the context. Match them with their definitions.

a. I thought my team would win, but it didn't **turn out** that way.

b. There are lots of things happening after school that students can **take part in**.

c. Chocolate is very **popular** in Switzerland.

d. The **opposite** of *popular* is *unpopular*.

e. **In general**, his parents don't let him stay out after midnight.

Target Word or Phrase	Definition
1. ____popular____ =	liked by many people
2. _____ =	happen or end in a specific way, have a specific result
3. _____ =	usually
4. _____ =	be active in a sport, club, or other event with other people
5. _____ =	a thing that is as different as can be from something else

> **Vocabulary Tip:**
> *Opposite* can be a noun: *What is the opposite of* bored? *Opposite* can also be an adjective: *The words* bored *and* excited *have opposite meanings.*

Building on the Vocabulary

Word Grammar: Verbs

Every sentence needs a **verb**. Most verbs are words for actions. For example, *run, fly, dance,* and *play* are verbs. The words *have, know,* and *be* are also verbs. They are nonaction verbs.

A verb can have more than one part: *can dance, has been working,* and *don't talk,* for example.

A **phrasal verb** has two parts, a verb and a particle. The meaning of a phrasal verb can be very different from the meaning of the verb alone. *Figure out, turn into,* and *turn out* are phrasal verbs.

Circle the verb in each sentence. Remember: A verb can be more than one word.

1. He (is) a professional tennis player.

2. (Don't mention) it.

3. First, melt the butter.

4. He is hiding the candy from the children.

5. I'm lonely.

6. Please share this with your brother.

7. They can't afford it.

8. Everything turned out fine in the end.

DEVELOPING YOUR READING SKILLS

Understanding Text Features

Text Features: Uses of Italics and Boldfacing in this Text

A feature is a part of something, often an important part. **Text features** are added to a text to help readers understand it. Two of the text features in this book are **boldfacing** and *italics*.

Uses of Boldfacing and Italics in *Password 3*	Examples
1. In the readings, the words in **bold** are the target vocabulary.	"They want a **specific** kind of food" (paragraph 1).
2. In other places, the writer may use **boldfacing** to introduce a new topic.	"A **phrasal verb** has two parts, a verb and a particle" (page 18).
3. Words are in *italics* when they're the topic of discussion.	"The opposite of *popular* is *unpopular.*"
4. Italics are also used to stress that a word is important.	"But the number one U.S. comfort food was *not* soft or warm" (paragraph 4).

> **Vocabulary Tip:** *Text* can mean a book or another piece of writing. The reading "Comfort Food" is a text. *Text* can also mean the words in a piece of writing (not the pictures).

Read each sentence. Why is the writer using boldfacing or italics? On the line, write the number of the reason from the chart (1, 2, 3, or 4).

1. Jacques says that as a boy, when he bit into one of his favorite chocolates, "That was *heaven!*" (page 3). ____

2. "The results of the survey were **rather** surprising" (page 14). ____

3. "Learn what *comfort food* means to different people" (page 13). ____

4. "Every sentence needs a **verb**" (page 18). ____

Scanning

Read the questions about "Comfort Food." Scan the reading and write the answers.

1. What is comfort food? Complete this definition with words taken from paragraph 2.

   Comfort food is food that helps people relax. It's "easy __*to prepare*__ and
   (a)

   easy _____." Eating comfort food gives people "a _____
   (b)   (c)

   feeling," and it "makes people feel 'Somebody's _____.'".
   (d)

2. How many people took part in the survey described in the reading? _____

3. What were the researchers' two main questions?

   a. _____

   b. _____

4. Who thinks of miso soup and soba noodles as comfort foods?

   _____

5. Who especially likes ice cream? _____

6. What two examples does the writer give of healthy, homemade comfort foods?

   _____

7. How are men's and women's comfort food choices different?

   _____

> **Reading Tip:** Watch for definitions when you read. In "Comfort Food," the writer asks, "What is comfort food?" and then explains it in several sentences.

Using Graphs and Charts

Complete the bar graph about U.S. men with information from the reading. Write the kinds of food men mentioned and the percentages of men in the survey who mentioned them. Then draw a bar graph with information for U.S women. Draw the bars and give the percentages.

Survey Results

%	Men	Women
100		
90		
80		
70		
60	ice cream 77%	
50		
40		
30		
20		
10		

Critical Thinking Tip: When you look at graphs and charts, you can see relationships between pieces of information. For example, it's easy to compare numbers.

Main Ideas

A. What is the main idea of the reading? Check ☑ your answer.

- ☐ 1. When you're feeling sad or lonely, what you need is comfort food.
- ☐ 2. *Comfort food* can mean sweet or salty snack foods or healthy, homemade foods.
- ☐ 3. Different people choose different comfort foods, but it's always food that makes them feel good.

B. What is the main idea of paragraph 6 in the reading? Check ☑ your answer.

- ☐ 1. Stress makes people want to eat comfort foods.
- ☐ 2. People want comfort food most when they are already feeling good.
- ☐ 3. The researchers wanted to know when people usually eat.

Critical Thinking Tip: To find the main idea of a paragraph, ask, *What is the topic of this paragraph? What is the most important information about that topic?*

CRITICAL THINKING

Discussion

Talk about these questions in a small group.

1. The reading says, "It's natural for people to eat when they are hungry, but people eat for other reasons, too" (paragraph 1). What other reasons does the writer mention? Which one do you think is most common? Do you disagree with any of the reasons mentioned? Explain.

2. Name your favorite comfort foods. Then go back to paragraph 2 and reread the definition for *comfort food*. How well does this definition describe your comfort foods? Explain your answer.

3. The writer calls the results of the survey "rather surprising" (paragraph 3). What surprised the researchers about the most popular comfort food in the United States? What was surprising about *when* people want comfort food? When do you think you most want your own comfort foods?

4. Take a survey in your group. How many people's favorite comfort foods are sweet? How many people's favorite comfort foods are salty? Compare the survey results for your group with the survey results reported in paragraph 5. Were your results the same as what the researchers found for U.S. men and women?

WRITING

A. Use the Target Vocabulary: Choose five target words or phrases from the list on pages 15–16. On a piece of paper, use each word or phrase in a sentence. Underline the target vocabulary. Then find a partner and read each other's sentences.

Examples:

> I wanted to see a movie last weekend, so I <u>mentioned</u> the idea to my friends.
> I didn't <u>expect</u> my classmates to sing "Happy Birthday" to me.

B. Practice Writing: Choose one of these topics and write a short paragraph about it. Then find a partner and read each other's paragraphs.

1. When do you feel bored, lonely, or under stress? What do you do to feel better?

2. The reading says people often want comfort foods when they have something to celebrate. When you have something to celebrate, what do you like to do?

Writing Tip: Some writers find it helps to talk about their ideas before they start writing. Try talking with a classmate about your topic before you write.

> When I feel lonely, I call a friend or someone in my family. Talking usually helps me feel better. Sometimes nobody answers the phone, and then I feel bad, but I leave messages for them. I try not to stay in my room by myself. I take my homework and go someplace where there are other people. Maybe I will talk to somebody, or maybe not. But I think it is a better way to pass the time when I feel lonely.

CHAPTER 3

The Love Apple

Beautiful and delicious

LEARNING OUTCOME

❯ Learn about the history of the tomato

GETTING READY TO READ

Talk about these questions with a partner.

1. What are tomatoes?

    a. vegetables   c. berries

    b. fruit   d. all of the above

2. People use tomatoes to prepare many different dishes. How many can you name? Make a list.

_____   _____

_____   _____

_____   _____

_____   _____

_____   _____

Read to Find Out: Where does the story of the tomato begin?

Look at the words and definitions next to the reading. Then read without stopping. Don't worry about new words. Don't stop to use a dictionary. Just keep reading.

The Love Apple

1　Ah, the tomato, so well-loved by foodies[1] everywhere! The French used to call it *la pomme d'amour*, "the love apple." Today, cooks around the world do wonderful things with it. There are more than 4,000 types of tomatoes and **no doubt** even more ways to eat them. Without the tomato, we would have no Mexican salsa or Italian pizza. Many wonderful Indian dishes would not be the same. After the potato, it's the most popular vegetable in the world. But wait—is it a vegetable?

2　You may be thinking, "Who cares?" But this question was **once** important enough that it had to be decided by the highest court in the United States. It happened back in 1893. At that time, there was a **tax** on vegetables brought into the country but no tax on imported[2] fruit. **Naturally,** importers of tomatoes called them fruit so as not to pay the tax. Not everyone agreed, and the question went all the way to the Supreme Court. The justices[3] knew that the tomato really is a fruit. That's because it's the part of the plant holding the **seeds**. To be more specific, the tomato is a berry. However, most people **considered** it a vegetable. They usually cooked and ate tomatoes more like vegetables than like fruit. That was the **basis** for the Court's decision in the **case**. The justices said that the tomato should be called—and taxed as—a vegetable.

3　The story of the tomato really begins much earlier. It starts in South America, where tomatoes grew wild. The first people to grow them were the Maya people of Central America. In the 1500s, the Spanish took tomatoes from Mexico to Spain. From there, tomatoes went to France, Italy, and other **areas** around the Mediterranean Sea. Those first tomatoes were small and yellow. Their color gave the tomato its Italian name, *pomodoro*, or *pomo d'oro*, "golden apple."

4　Europeans did not fall in love with tomatoes quickly. For a long time, they were afraid to eat them. The tomato plant looks like a plant called deadly nightshade, or belladonna, and is part of the same family. The **roots**, leaves, and berries of the deadly nightshade are **highly** poisonous.[4] So it took a while for Europeans to **accept** the tomato. A cookbook with tomato recipes[5] did not become **available** to the public until 1692.

[1] *foodie* = (informal) a person who knows about and loves good food

[2] *imported* = brought into a country to sell

[3] *justices* = judges

[4] *poisonous* = very dangerous to eat or drink

[5] *recipe* = a set of instructions for cooking something

5   By the late 1700s, Europeans were happily eating tomatoes. However, in the United States, most people did not yet trust them. President Thomas Jefferson (1743–1826) helped to **change their minds**. He grew tomatoes in his gardens and **served** them at dinners in the White House. Today, tomatoes are so popular in the U.S. that 85 percent of home gardeners grow them. As every one of those gardeners would no doubt tell you, there's nothing like a fresh homegrown tomato.

Quick Comprehension Check

A. Read these sentences **about the reading**. Circle T (true) or F (false). On the line, write the number of the paragraph with the answer.

1. Cooks use tomatoes in many different parts of the world.   T   F   _____
2. The tomato is a kind of fruit.   T   F   _____
3. Tomatoes were called vegetables by U.S. law.   T   F   _____
4. The first tomatoes grew in Italy.   T   F   _____
5. A U.S. president introduced tomatoes to Europe.   T   F   _____
6. The tomato plant looks like a plant that might kill you.   T   F   _____

B. Work with your class. Share your answers from part A. Go back to the reading to find the reason why a statement is true or false. Correct the false statements.

EXPLORING VOCABULARY

Thinking about the Target Vocabulary

A. Look at the chart with the target vocabulary. Three verbs are missing. Scan the reading to find the three verbs in **bold**. Add them to the correct places in the chart. Write the base form of each verb.

> **Vocabulary Tip:** The **base form** of a verb is the simple form without any endings on it, like the verbs *be*, *go*, and *have*. When you look for a verb in the dictionary, look for the base form.

¶	Nouns	Verbs	Adjectives	Other
1				no doubt
2				once
	tax			
				naturally
	seed			

¶	Nouns	Verbs	Adjectives	Other
	basis			
	case			
3	area			
4	root			
				highly
			available	
5				change someone's mind

B. Which words and phrases are new to you? Circle them in the chart. Then find them in the reading. Look at the context. Can you guess the meaning?

Reading Tip: Read first for the main ideas. Don't stop reading to use your dictionary. Read again for a better understanding, and use your dictionary as needed.

Using the Target Vocabulary

A. These sentences are **about the reading**. Complete them with the words and phrases in the box.

accept	basis	change their minds	highly	once
available	case	consider	no doubt	served

1. There are more than 4,000 types of tomatoes. You can be sure that there are even more ways to eat them. _____ there are thousands of ways.

2. "Is the tomato a vegetable or a fruit?" This question was _____ (at some time in the past) so important that the U.S. Supreme Court had to make the decision.

3. Most people in the United States think of the tomato as a vegetable. They don't _____ it a fruit.

4. The Supreme Court justices looked at the way most U.S. cooks used

   tomatoes. That was the _____ of their decision. They used

   that as the reason for their decision.

5. The justices called the tomato a vegetable. That was their decision

   in the _____.

6. The fruit of the deadly nightshade is very dangerous. It is

   _____ poisonous.

Vocabulary Tip: In the reading, *case* means a specific problem or question that is decided in a court of law. *Case* has other meanings, too. Check your dictionary for more information.

7. Europeans at first did not believe that tomatoes were good to eat. It took

   a long time for them to _____ this idea.

8. Tomatoes arrived in Europe in the 1500s, but many years passed before

   people began cooking with them. The first cookbook explaining how to

   use tomatoes became _____ for people to buy in 1692.

9. In the late 1700s, most people in the United States did not trust the

   tomato. Then President Thomas Jefferson helped to _____.

   People started to see tomatoes differently.

10. Jefferson had dishes made with tomatoes for his guests at White House

    dinners. He _____ tomatoes to his guests.

B. These sentences use the target words and phrases **in new contexts**. Complete them with the words and phrases in the box.

accept	basis	changed my mind	highly	once
available	cases	consider	no doubt	served

1. Jennifer is very important to me. I _____ her one of my best

   friends.

2. Some court _____ are decided by a judge, and some are

   decided by a jury—a group of people like you and me.

3. When we got to the restaurant, it was very busy. We had to wait for a

   table to become _____.

4. He doesn't want to see her anymore. I know it hurts, but she can't do anything about it. She'll have to _____ it.

5. Be careful! It says "_____ flammable." That means it can catch fire very easily.

6. Let's call her. It's already ten o'clock, and she gets up early, so _____ she's awake.

7. It's a vegetarian restaurant. That means they don't _____ meat.

8. I used to think chocolate was bad for you, but I've _____.

9. The idea that tomatoes were dangerous to eat had no _____ in fact.

10. I _____ expected them to get married, but I don't anymore.

C. Read the sentences. Guess the meaning of the **boldfaced** target words and phrases from the context. Match them with their definitions.

a. Can they move that tree, or are the **roots** too deep?

b. When I cook with tomatoes, I don't use the **seeds**.

c. The team lost the big game, so **naturally**, they all feel bad.

d. You have to add the 5 percent sales **tax** to the price.

e. My family couldn't afford a house in that **area**.

Target Word		**Definition**
1. _____	=	in a way that you would expect
2. _____	=	a part of a place, city, country, etc.
3. _____	=	small hard objects produced by plants, from which a new plant can grow
4. _____	=	the parts of a plant or tree that grow under the ground
5. _____	=	money you have to pay to the government based on what you buy, how much money you make, where you live, etc.

> **Vocabulary Tip:** *Etc.* is short for the Latin phrase *et cetera*. This abbreviation is often used at the end of a list. It means "and other people or things of the same kind."

Building on the Vocabulary

Word Grammar: Adjectives

An **adjective** is a word that describes

a person:	a *popular* boy, *fast* runners
a place:	*beautiful* cities, a *large* airport
a thing:	*tall* windows, *small* cars
an idea:	*new* information, a *nice* surprise

An adjective can come before a noun: *I have* **good friends**.

An adjective can follow the verb *be, get,* or *feel*: *Mary and John* **are happy**. *Please* **get ready**. *I* **feel tired**.

Adjectives have no plural form.

Circle the adjective in each sentence.

1. It's not (expensive)
2. My computer gets dusty.
3. It was just an average day.
4. She is a professional musician.

5. Do you think he's lonely?
6. I have a specific color in mind.
7. It is natural for babies to cry sometimes.
8. What do you do when you feel bored?

DEVELOPING YOUR READING SKILLS

Scanning

Read these questions. Scan "The Love Apple" and write short answers.

1. Who called the tomato "the love apple"? _____

2. What are three examples of countries where tomatoes are an important food?

   _____   _____   _____

3. In what year did the U.S. Supreme Court make its tomato decision? _____

4. Where did the first wild tomatoes grow? _____

5. Where did people first plant them? _____

6. What is deadly nightshade? _____

7. What was the date of the first European cookbook with tomato recipes?

   _____

8. Who was Thomas Jefferson? _____

Understanding Cause and Effect

Complete the sentences. Find the causes in the reading.

1. The tomato is really a fruit because _____.

2. The Supreme Court decided to call the tomato a vegetable because

   _____.

3. In the 1600s, people in Europe were afraid to eat tomatoes because

   _____.

4. In the 1800s, people in the United States began eating tomatoes in part

   because _____.

Summarizing

Writing a Summary of a Reading

A **summary** is a short report on a longer reading. It has only the main information. When you summarize a reading, you have to think about which ideas matter most and figure out how to put them into writing. Summarizing helps you understand, remember, and talk about the information.

Complete this summary of the reading. Write one or more words in each blank.

The tomato is a _____, but many people consider it a
                      (1)

_____. It is the second most _____ in
        (2)   (3)

_____. Tomatoes first grew in _____ and traveled
        (4)   (5)

from there to _____. People in Europe and the United
                        (6)

States did not accept them at first because they were afraid that

_____.
                              (7)

CRITICAL THINKING

Discussion

Talk about these questions with the whole class.

Critical Thinking Tip: The **purpose** of a sentence or paragraph is the reason why it is in the reading. Is it there to give the writer's opinion? Does it give an example or explain why something is true?

1. What is the purpose of the first paragraph? Choose the best answer.

    a. to let the reader know that the writer is a foodie

    b. to compare the tomato with other vegetables

    c. to introduce the idea that people care a lot about tomatoes

    Explain why you chose your answer.

2. Why does the writer use the word *naturally* in paragraph 2? What does the writer think is natural? Do you agree?

3. How long did it take from the time the tomato arrived in Europe until it became popular there? What is one reason that people were slow to accept it?

4. The world has changed in many ways since the introduction of the tomato. Do you think that people today are quicker to accept food from other places? Explain your answer. Can you give examples of foods from other countries that you have learned to like?

5. The reading says that in Italian, a tomato is *un pomodoro*. Why did the Italians give it this name? The reading also says that the French used to call the tomato *la pomme d'amour*, meaning "the love apple." Does the reading explain why? Why do you think it got this name?

6. What are "homegrown" tomatoes? How does the writer feel about them? Do you agree? If you love tomatoes, what is your favorite way to eat them?

WRITING

A. Use the Target Vocabulary: Choose five target words or phrases from the chart on pages 25–26. On a piece of paper, use each word or phrase in a sentence. Then find a partner and read each other's sentences.

B. Practice Writing: Choose one of these topics and write a short paragraph about it. Then find a partner and read each other's paragraphs.

1. People often have foods that they think they could not live without. What favorite food do you feel that strongly about? Why is it so important to you? You can begin: *I could not live without...*

Writing Tip: After you write a paragraph, take a break. Look at it again an hour later—or better still, the next day. That will help you see ways to make it better.

2. Is there a food that others like but you would never eat? Explain how you feel about this food and why. You can begin: *Some people consider... good to eat, but I do not.*

CHAPTER 4

Slow Food

LEARNING OUTCOME

❯ Learn about the Slow Food movement

A traditional meal to enjoy

GETTING READY TO READ

Talk about these questions with your class.

1. What is fast food? Write a definition: Fast food is food that

   _____.

2. How many examples of fast food can you think of in 30 seconds? Make a list.

3. What's good about fast food? What's bad about fast food? Make two lists.

4. What do you think the phrase *slow food* means?

READING

Read to Find Out: What are the members of Slow Food worried about?

Look at the picture, words, and definitions next to the reading. Then read without stopping. Don't worry about new words. Don't stop to use a dictionary. Just keep reading.

Slow Food

1   Italians know and love good food. It's at the heart of their **culture**. So is taking the time to enjoy their food. They do not like to **rush** through meals. As a result, many of them think that fast food is a **terrible** idea.

2   In 1986, the first American fast-food restaurant—a McDonald's—opened in Rome. Many Italians were surprised and angry. They saw it as an **attack** on Italian culture. One man, Carlo Petrini, decided to fight back. "Fast food is the **enemy**," he said, and he started a group called Slow Food. Today, over 100,000 people in 160 countries belong to the group. More people **join** every day.

3   The **members** of Slow Food share many of the same ideas about problems with food today. One of those problems is fast food. Slow Food members consider it unhealthy. They also do not like that fast food is the same everywhere. "That's **boring**," they say. What is better are healthy, **local** food traditions with all their wonderful **variety**.

4   Slow Food members worry about a second problem, too. For a variety of reasons, some types of plants and animals are becoming very rare.[1] Some have become so rare that the world is in **danger** of losing them completely. Some examples are:

- Several kinds of dates that grow only in the area around Siwa, Egypt;

- The blue-egg chickens of Temuco, Chile, who **produce** eggs only when they live outside;

- The wild coffee plants of the Harenna Forest in Ethiopia, the only place in the world where you can find coffee plants in the wild; and

- The pirarucù, a fish in the Amazon River that can **weigh** more than 500 pounds (as much as 250 kilograms).

  Slow Food does not want to let these plants and animals **disappear**, so the organization[2] is working with

Picking Siwa dates

[1] *rare* = unusual and hard to find

[2] *organization* = a group, such as a club or business, formed for a specific reason

local groups to stop that from happening. Slow Food wants to protect biodiversity—the wide variety of types of plants and animals we have on Earth.

5   There is a third problem that worries Slow Food members. Much of our food today is produced by big companies. These companies sell their products in distant places, so they want products that can travel well. Big growers[3] want the kinds of fruit and vegetables that look good after a long trip. But how do their apples, lettuce, and tomatoes taste when they finally arrive? That is less important to them. So now we have more trouble finding good-tasting fresh fruit and vegetables.

[3] big growers = large farm companies

6   Today, it has become common to eat foods from far away. Foods eaten in the United States travel an average of 1,300 miles to **reach** the dinner table. In the past, people got most of their food from farms in their local area. Slow Food members say, "People should be buying more local food. It's fresh, and it's part of our culture." One man in the United States, Gary Nabhan, decided to try this. For one year, all his food came from plants and animals near his home in Arizona. One local animal there is the rattlesnake.[4] Nabhan ate that, too! In his book *Coming Home to Eat*, he says it tastes just like chicken.

[4] a rattlesnake

7   Fast food is reaching more and more parts of the world. But Slow Food is getting its message to more and more people, too.

Quick Comprehension Check

A. Read these sentences **about the reading**. Circle T (true) or F (false). On the line, write the number of the paragraph with the answer.

1. Good food is an important part of everyday life in Italy.   T   F   ____

2. The group Slow Food opened a McDonald's in Rome.   T   F   ____

3. Slow Food members say fast food is not interesting or healthy.   T   F   ____

4. Slow Food members say food from far away is too expensive.   T   F   ____

5. Slow Food members worry about rare plants and animals.   T   F   ____

6. Slow Food members want everyone to eat Italian food.   T   F   ____

B. Work with your class. Share your answers from part A. Go back to the reading to find the reason why a sentence is true or false. Correct the false sentences.

EXPLORING VOCABULARY

Thinking about the Target Vocabulary

A. Look at the chart with the target vocabulary. Three adjectives are missing. Scan the reading to find the three adjectives in **bold**. Add them to the correct places in the chart.

¶	Nouns	Verbs	Adjectives	Other
1	culture			
		rush		
2	attack			
	enemy			
		join		
3	member			
	variety			
4	danger			
		produce		
		weigh		
		disappear		
6		reach		

B. Which words are new to you? Circle them in the chart. Then find the words in the reading. Look at the context. Can you guess the meaning?

> **Vocabulary Tip:** You will not always be able to guess a word's meaning from its context. Sometimes you will need to look for it in a dictionary.

Using the Target Vocabulary

A. These sentences are **about the reading**. Complete them with the words in the box.

boring	join	produce	rush	weigh
disappear	local	reach	variety	

1. Italians don't want to hurry at mealtime. They don't like to

   _____ through meals.

2. The group Slow Food is growing. More people _____ the group every day.

3. If food becomes the same everywhere, it will be less interesting. It will

   be _____.

4. When people eat food that is grown near where they live, they are eating

   _____ food.

5. The group Slow Food wants there to be many different types of food.

   They want _____ in food.

6. There are some very unusual chickens in Temuco, Chile. They

   _____ blue eggs.

7. The pirarucù can grow very big and get very heavy. It can

   _____over 500 pounds.

8. Some kinds of plants and animals are now very few in number. They may go away completely. Slow Food doesn't want these plants and animals to

   _____.

9. Food often travels far before it gets to our homes. It may travel many

   miles to _____ your dinner table.

> **Vocabulary Tip:**
> When you learn a new word, it is a good idea to learn other words in the same word family. The verb *produce* is related to the noun *product* and the adjective *productive*.

B. These sentences use the target words **in new contexts**. Complete them with the words in the box.

boring	joined	produces	rushing	weighed
disappeared	local	reach	variety	

1. The baby _____ nine pounds when he was born.

2. The newspaper gives both the national weather and our

   _____ weather.

3. The plane will be taking off on time, so we should _____ Tokyo on time.

4. Farmers in California grow a wide _____ of vegetables.

5. Don't worry. We have lots of time. Slow down and stop _____ around!

6. What a _____ movie! It almost put me to sleep.

7. Last month, Tomas _____ an athletic club. Now he goes there to exercise.

8. There are no more dodos in the world. The last of these birds

   _____ several hundred years ago.

9. Argentina _____ a lot of meat, wheat, and corn.

C. Read each definition and look at the paragraph number. Look back at the reading on pages 33–34 to find the **boldfaced** word to match the definition. Copy it in the chart.

Definition	Paragraph	Target Word
1. the ideas, beliefs, art, and behavior of a specific society or group of people.	1	
2. very, very bad	1	
3. a violent act to try to hurt someone or something	2	
4. someone you are fighting in a war; the opposite of *friend*	2	
5. people who belong to a group or club	3	
6. the chance that someone or something will be hurt	4	

Vocabulary Tip: The noun *danger* is a member of the same word family as the adjective *dangerous* and the verb *endanger* (meaning to put someone or something in danger).

Building on the Vocabulary

> **Word Grammar: Adjectives Ending in -ing and -ed**
>
> There are many pairs of adjectives that end in -ing and -ed.
>
> - The -ed adjective usually describes a person. It tells how someone feels: *I was surprised to hear the news.*
> - The -ing adjective describes the thing that causes the feeling: *They told us some surprising news.*
> - The -ing adjective can also describe a person: *He's a boring speaker. I get bored listening to him.*

A. Complete the sentences. Use each adjective only once.

1. (surprising, surprised) It was _____ news. Everyone was

   (a)

   _____.

   (b)

2. (boring, bored) What a _____ class! I was completely

   (a)

   _____.

   (b)

3. (interesting, interested) He's _____ in learning to cook. Food

   (a)

   is very _____ to him.

   (b)

4. (exciting, excited) I'm _____ about my vacation. It's going

   (a)

   to be _____.

   (b)

5. (tiring, tired) I'm _____. Today was a _____ day.

   (a)   (b)

B. Write four sentences. Use -ed and -ing adjectives.

1. _____

2. _____

3. _____

4. _____

DEVELOPING YOUR READING SKILLS

Understanding Text Features

Text Features: Photos, Illustrations, Titles, and Captions

Most of the information in a text is found in the writer's sentences, but text features also carry meaning. The **title** of a text helps you understand what it will be about. **Photos** (short for *photographs*) and **illustrations** (or drawings) help you picture what the writer is saying. **Captions** tell you what you are seeing in a photo or illustration. The caption usually goes under the photo or illustration.

Complete the statements. Write *caption, illustration, photo,* or *title*.

1. The _____ of the reading in this chapter is "Slow Food."

2. On page 32, the _____ shows what "a traditional meal" looks like.

3. The _____ under the photo on page 33 is "Picking Siwa dates."

4. On page 34, there is an _____ of a rattlesnake.

> **Reading Tip:** Text features can help you understand a reading. They often add to or explain the information in the text itself. Look at them before you read.

Scanning

Read the questions below. Then go back to the reading and scan it for the answers.

1. How do Italians feel about good food? _____

2. What happened in Rome in 1986? _____

3. Who is Carlo Petrini? _____

4. What three problems worry the members of Slow Food?

   a. _____

   b. _____

   c. _____

5. Why don't some fruits and vegetables taste good?

_____

> **Writing Tip:** You can answer some questions by copying phrases and sentences from the reading. Show that you're using a phrase or sentence from the reading by putting quotation marks (" ") before and after it.

6. How far does food travel (on average) in the United States? _____

7. What do Slow Food members think about local food?

_____

8. What did Gary Nabhan do?

_____

Main Ideas

A. What is the main idea of "Slow Food"? Check ☑ your answer.

☐ 1. Slow Food members want everyone to be able to enjoy a variety of healthy, local foods.

☐ 2. The group Slow Food is working to put an end to fast-food restaurants.

☐ 3. The group Slow Food began in Rome because of an attack on Italian culture.

B. What is the main idea of paragraph 2 in the reading? Check ☑ your answer.

☐ 1. In 1986, a McDonald's restaurant opened in Rome, Italy.

☐ 2. Fast-food restaurants have become more and more popular in Italy.

☐ 3. The group Slow Food began as a way to fight back against fast-food.

CRITICAL THINKING

Discussion

Talk about these questions in a small group.

1. The reading says that good food is "at the heart of" Italian culture (paragraph 1). What does the phrase *at the heart of* mean? The reading also says that Italians believe in taking the time to eat without rushing. That is not the case in some other cultures. Is it true of your culture? Explain your answer.

2. How would a member of Slow Food compare slow food with fast food? Tell at least three ways that they are different. Underline information in the reading that supports your answers.

3. With your group, complete columns **a** and **b** in the chart with information from the reading. On your own, complete column **c** with your ideas. If you do not agree that something is a problem, then in column **c**, you can write "Nothing." Share your ideas for column **c** with your group.

	a. Problems that worry Slow Food members	b. Why Slow Food says it's a problem	c. What to do about it
1			
2			
3			

4. Do a role-play in your group. Imagine that one or two of you are members of Slow Food. The other one or two of you are TV reporters who eat fast food every day. The reporters start asking questions. For example, they can ask the Slow Food members about their group, their ideas about food, and what they eat. The Slow Food members answer the questions and also ask the reporters questions of their own.

> **Critical Thinking Tip:** You must use critical thinking skills to take part in a role-play. Think about the person whose role you are playing. What opinions do they hold? What would they say?

WRITING

A. Use the Target Vocabulary: Choose five target words or phrases from the chart on page 35. On a piece of paper, use each word or phrase in a sentence. Underline the target vocabulary. Then find a partner and read each other's sentences.

B. Practice Writing: Choose one of these topics and write about it. Then find a partner and read each other's work.

1. Are you a member of any group? It could be a club, a religious group, a sports team, or a group of any type. Write a paragraph about your experience. Describe the group, and tell when and why you joined it.

2. Write a conversation between a reporter and a Slow Food member or a fast-food lover. Have the reporter ask four or more questions. You can begin:

> REPORTER: Excuse me. Can I ask you some questions about food?
>
> FAST-FOOD LOVER: Sure.

Checkpoint

LOOK BACK

A. Think About This

Look back at your answers to the *Think About This* question on page 1:

How do you choose the food you eat?

Do you want to change any of your answers? Do you want to add anything new?

B. Remember the Readings

What do you want to remember most from the readings in Unit 1? For each chapter, write one sentence about the reading.

Chapter 1: Crazy about Chocolate

_____

Chapter 2: Comfort Food

_____

Chapter 3: The Love Apple

_____

Chapter 4: Slow Food

_____

REVIEWING VOCABULARY

A. Match the words with their definitions. There are two extra words.

accept	boring	expect	reach
bored	disappear	offer	suggest

1. _____ = become impossible to see or find

2. _____ = arrive at or get to a place

3. _____ = believe that something will happen

4. _____ = not interesting in any way

5. _____ = decide that someone or something is good enough

6. _____ = tell someone your ideas about what they should do

B. Complete the sentences with the phrases. There is one extra phrase.

changed my mind	get to	no doubt	turn out
figuring out	in general	take part	turn it into

1. John said nothing. He didn't _____ in the conversation.

2. Barbara is very good at _____ crossword puzzles.

3. Maria has already changed her mind twice. She always changes her mind and _____ she'll do it again.

4. I wanted to visit Hollywood on my trip to California, but I didn't _____ do that. There wasn't enough time.

5. Chris and Pat are preparing to take one of the bedrooms in their house and _____ a home office.

6. I fell asleep during the movie. How did the story _____?

7. We might have some cool nights, but _____, the weather is warm at this time of year.

EXPANDING VOCABULARY

> ## Word Families
>
> Each form of a word belongs to the same word family. For example, the noun *specifics*, the verb *specify*, and the adjective *specific* are all members of the same word family.
>
> Sometimes two members of a word family look the same. That is true for the words *attack*, *mention*, *rush*, and *share*—they can be nouns or verbs.

A. The pairs of words in parentheses are members of the same word family. Circle the correct word to complete the sentence. Write *noun* or *verb*.

1. a. You are free to (choice / choose) the courses you want.   _verb_

    b. He made the (choice / choose) to return to school.   _____

2. a. I like (variety / vary) in my food.   _____

    b. The dishes on the menu (variety / vary) from day to day.   _____

3. a. How much did the baby (weight / weigh)?   _____

    b. The nurse checked my (weight / weigh).   _____

4. a. What did the scientists (finding / find)?   _____

    b. He considered it the most important (finding / find) of his research.   _____

5. a. What was the (basis / base) for their disagreement?   _____

    b. The director will (basis / base) his next movie on a comic book.   _____

B. What part of speech is the **boldfaced** word? Circle *n.* for *noun* or *v.* for *verb*.

1. I didn't hear any **mention** of taxes when the president spoke.   *n.*   *v.*

2. The dog made a lot of noise, but it didn't **attack**.   *n.*   *v.*

3. His **share** is the same size as his brother's.   *n.*   *v.*

4. Don't be in such a **rush**—we have lots of time.   *n.*   *v.*

A PUZZLE

Complete the sentences with words you studied in Chapters 1–4. Write the words in the puzzle.

ACROSS

2. The café doesn't _____*serve*_____ dinner, only breakfast and lunch.

5. Locally-grown tomatoes are _____ only in late summer.

6. Donna took her _____ to court and she won.

9. I want to buy a car, but I don't have a _____ kind of car in mind.

11. The _____ of *terrible* is *wonderful*.

12. Naturally, my aunt felt _____ after her husband died.

DOWN

1. You can watch a lot of _____ sports on TV.

3. Peter is 5 foot 11, _____ 6 feet tall.

4. When the sun comes out, the ice will _____.

7. The _____ person needs 7.5 hours sleep a night.

8. The cats like to _____ in the tall grass.

10. We need to clean the house. Everything is _____.

BUILDING DICTIONARY SKILLS

Finding Words in the Dictionary

Guidewords

Guidewords help you find words in the dictionary. Guidewords are the words at the top of dictionary pages. The word at the top of the left page is the first word on the left page. The word at the top of the right page is the last word on the right page.

A. Below are the tops of two dictionary pages. Look at the guidewords on these pages.

1. What is the first word you would find a definition

    for on page 300? _____

2. What is the last word you would find a definition

    for on page 301? _____

doorman	300
door•man /'dɔrmæn, -mən/ *n* plural doormen /-mɛn, -mən/ [C] a man who works at the door of a hotel or theater, helping people who are coming in or out	
door•mat /'dɔrmæt/ *n* [C] 1 a thick piece of material just outside a door for you to clean your shoes on	

301	doubtful
because you are surprised by what you originally saw or heard	
'double-talk' *n* [U] *disapproving* speech that is complicated, and is intended to deceive or confuse people	
'double' vision *n* [U] a medical condition in which you see two of . . .	

B. The guidewords for pages 300–301 are *doorman* and *doubtful*. Read the words below. Will these words be on pages 300–301? Check ☑ Yes or No.

	Yes	No
1. dot	☐	☐
2. double	☐	☐
3. doll	☐	☐
4. doubt	☐	☐
5. doughnut	☐	☐
6. dorm	☐	☐

Alphabetizing Compound Words

A **compound word** is made up of two words. Some compound words are written as one word (*birthday, homework*); others are written as two words (*ice cream, good night*); and others are written with a hyphen (*good-looking, bird-brained*). The *Longman Dictionary of American English* treats these words as one word and lists them with other words in alphabetical order, for example:

good

good evening

good-for-nothing

goodwill

Write the following words in the order you would expect to find them in the dictionary.

ice cream   ice-cold   ice

icebreaker   ice cap   ice cream cone

1. _____   4. _____

2. _____   5. _____

3. _____   6. _____

Words with Superscripts

Words in the dictionary sometimes have **superscripts**. A superscript is a small, raised number, like this: [2]. When a word in the dictionary has a superscript, it means that the word can be more than one part of speech and there is more than one entry for the word. It's usually a good idea to read all the meanings and uses of the word.

A. Look at the dictionary entries for *local[1]* and *local.[2]* What part of speech is *local?* Complete the sentence.

Local can be an _____ or a _____.

> **lo•cal**[1] /ˈloʊkəl/ *adj* **1** [usually before noun] relating to a particular place or area, especially the place you live in: *a good local hospital* | *The story appeared in the local newspaper.* | *It cost a quarter to make a **local call*** (= a telephone call to someone in the same area as you). **2** *technical* affecting a particular part of your body: *a local anesthetic*
>
> **local**[2] *n* **the locals** the people who live in a particular place

B. Look at the entries for *tax* and answer the questions.

---

tax[1] /tæks/ *n* [C,U] the money you must pay the government, based on how much you earn, what you buy, where you live, etc.: *a 13% **tax on** cigarettes* | *Everyone who works **pays tax.*** | *The city will have to **raise taxes** to pay for the roads.* | *If elected, she promised to **cut taxes.*** | *I only earn $25,000 a year **after taxes** (= after paying tax).* | *a **tax increase/cut***

tax[2] *v* [T] **1** to charge a tax on something: *Incomes of under $30,000 are **taxed at** 15%.* **2 tax sb's patience/ strength etc.** to use almost all of someone's PATIENCE, strength, etc.: *His constant questions had begun to tax her patience.*

---

1. How many entries does the dictionary have for *tax?* _____

2. What part of speech is *tax?*

    It can be a _____ or a _____ .

3. How many meanings does the dictionary give for *tax?* _____

LIFE CHANGES

THINK ABOUT THIS

Which of these life changes have you experienced?

Check ✔ your answers, and add ideas of your own.

- [ ] Moving to a new place to live
- [ ] Going to a new school
- [ ] Starting a new job
- [ ] Getting married
- [ ] Using a new language
- [ ] Other life changes: _____

CHAPTER 5

Life Is Full of Surprises

Mahmoud Arani in the classroom

LEARNING OUTCOME

❯ Learn about someone whose dreams had to change

GETTING READY TO READ

Talk about these questions with your class.

1. Mahmoud Arani is from Iran. Tell what you know about Iran.

2. Many people leave their countries to study or to work. Discuss some reasons why people do this.

READING

Read to Find Out: What big changes have happened in Mahmoud's life?

Look at the words and definitions next to the reading. Then read without stopping.

Life is Full of Surprises

1   Mahmoud Arani teaches at a small U.S. college. He did not expect to **end up** in the United States, and he did not expect to teach. He grew up in Iran, and he planned to become a doctor. However, as people say, life is full of surprises.

2   Mahmoud was born in Iran near the city of Tehran. In high school, he was an excellent student—the best in his class—and he was planning on a career in **medicine**. First, he had to take the national university entrance exam.[1] He needed to do well on the exam to be accepted by a medical school.[2] Out of 50,000 high school students taking the test, only 1,000 would get the chance to study medicine. Mahmoud missed the **score** he needed by a few points, which his teachers found very surprising. He took the test again, and again, he had to **deal with** bad news. "I was **disappointed**," he remembers, "but I said, 'That is my fate.'"[3]

3   Mahmoud had to make a new plan for his future, so he chose to study English. After college in Tehran, he decided to go to the United States for an advanced degree[4] in English. A few months later, he arrived in Buffalo, New York. He entered an English as a Second Language (ESL) program at the state university there. Mahmoud was one of about 500,000 **international** students who entered the United States to study that year, but he **managed to** do something that few others could do. In less than two years, he went from studying ESL to teaching it at the same school!

4   While on a visit home, Mahmoud had an **interview** at a university in Tehran. They offered him a teaching job, and he accepted it. Officials[5] at the university made an agreement with him: Mahmoud would return to Buffalo to finish his degree, and they would give him financial[6] **support**. After he finished, he would come back to teach. So Mahmoud went back to New York feeling great, believing that his future was **secure**.

5   Things did not turn out as he expected, however. There was a revolution[7] in Iran, which caused great changes in the country. Soon Mahmoud received a letter from his university in Tehran. It said, "We don't need any English teachers." **Suddenly**, his support was gone, and his future was unclear. It was **a shock**.

[1] *the national university entrance exam* = a test students in Iran took before they could enter college

[2] *medical school* = a program for teaching people to be doctors

[3] *fate* = the things that will happen that a person cannot choose

[4] *an advanced degree* = what someone gets for completing a masters or doctoral program at a university

[5] *officials* = the people running an organization or government

[6] *financial* = relating to money

[7] *revolution* = a time of great and sudden change in a country

6   Mahmoud decided not to **give up**. He continued studying for his degree, and after much hard work, he reached his goal. Soon he had a good job teaching at Saint Michael's College in Vermont.

7   Things have turned out well for Mahmoud. His students at Saint Michael's report that he is a great teacher. He is married, and he and his wife, Roya, have two children. Roya, who is also from Iran, is a doctor. Mahmoud has always been interested in medicine. "I could go to medical school now," he says, "if I had the **patience**!" He says that he does not plan to make a career change at this **stage** in his life. However, he adds, "I know that life is full of surprises."

Quick Comprehension Check

A. Read these sentences. Circle T (true) or F (false). On the line, write the number of the paragraph with the answer.

1. Mahmoud was born and grew up in Iran.   T   F   _____

2. Mahmoud planned to study medicine and become a doctor.   T   F   _____

3. He traveled to the United States to study medicine.   T   F   _____

4. He expected to have a job teaching at a university in Iran.   T   F   _____

5. The Iranian revolution happened while he was at home in Tehran.   T   F   _____

6. The revolution changed his life.   T   F   _____

B. Work with your class. Share your answers from part A. Go back to the reading to find the reason why a sentence is true or false. Correct the false sentences.

EXPLORING VOCABULARY

Thinking about the Target Vocabulary

A. Look at the chart with the target vocabulary. Four verbs are missing. Scan the reading to find them. Three of them are phrasal verbs. Add the verbs to the correct places in the chart. Write the base form of each verb.

¶	Nouns	Verbs	Adjectives	Other
1				
2	medicine			
	score			

¶	Nouns	Verbs	Adjectives	Other
			disappointed	
3			international	
4	interview			
	support			
			secure	
5				suddenly
	shock			
6				
7	patience			
	stage			

B. Which words are new to you? Circle them in the chart. Then find the words in the reading. Look at the context. Can you guess the meaning?

Using the Target Vocabulary

A. These sentences are **about the reading.** Complete them with the words and phrases in the box.

deal with	give up	managed to	patience	suddenly
disappointed	international	medicine	stage	support

1. Mahmoud wanted to study _____ so that he could become a doctor.

2. When Mahmoud got his test results, he had to _____ some bad news. He had to think about the problem and decide what to do about it.

3. Mahmoud says that he was _____ when he did not get the result he hoped for on his test. It is natural to feel that way when something does not turn out well.

> **Vocabulary Tip:**
> *Study medicine* means to learn the science of treating sick or hurt people. *Take medicine* means to eat or drink something that can help a sick person get well.

4. In the year that Mahmoud entered the United States to study, about half a million other _____ students did the same. These were students from countries around the world.

5. Mahmoud was able to do something difficult. He _____ do something that few international students could do.

6. The officials at the university in Tehran said they would help Mahmoud pay for his education in the United States. They promised him financial _____.

Vocabulary Tip:
Disappointed and *disappointing* form a pair of adjectives: *Mahmoud's test score was disappointing. Mahmoud was disappointed.* When you learn an adjective ending in *-ing* or *-ed*, find out if it is one of a pair.

7. Mahmoud wasn't expecting to lose his financial support. It happened _____.

8. It was hard for Mahmoud to keep going, but he didn't _____. He did not lose hope and he never stopped trying.

9. Mahmoud says that he could go to medical school now, but that would take a lot of _____. He didn't think he could wait several years for a medical degree.

10. At one time in the past, Mahmoud wanted to become a doctor. But at this _____ of his life, he is happy as a professor.

B. These sentences use the target words and phrases **in new contexts**. Complete them with the words and phrases in the box.

deal with	gave up	managed to	patience	suddenly
disappointed	international	medicine	stages	support

1. Parts of the ocean that do not belong to any one country are called _____ waters.

2. Children go through different _____ as they grow. Each one is a time of learning new skills, like learning to walk or talk, and later, learning to think like an adult.

3. I gave some money to the International Red Cross, and they thanked me for my _____.

Vocabulary Tip:
Support can be a noun or a verb. It has many meanings. See your dictionary to learn more.

4. Ben usually liked working at the restaurant but not when he had to
_____ difficult customers.

5. I kept leaving messages for you, but you never called me back, so
finally I _____ and stopped calling.

6. "Practice _____" means to work as a doctor, and "practice
law" means to work as a lawyer.

7. I forgot my house key, so I couldn't open the door, but I
_____ get in through a window.

8. Parents of small children need to have a lot of _____. They
have to speak quietly and not get angry.

9. She promised to help me, but then she changed her mind. Naturally, I
was _____.

10. We were eating dinner when _____, the lights went out.

C. Read the sentences. Guess the meaning of the **boldfaced** target words and
phrases from the context. Match them with their definitions.

a. I didn't get a good **score** on the test, so I was disappointed.
b. The news of the accident came as a **shock**.
c. He can relax and stop worrying about money. He has a **secure**
job now.
d. We got on the wrong train and **ended up** getting to the airport
late.
e. How will you prepare for your job **interview**?

> **Writing Tip:** Use
> *end up* + a place
> *(He ended up in the
> hospital)* or *end up*
> + an *-ing* verb *(They
> ended up winning
> the game).*

Target Word		Definition
1. _____	=	a formal meeting at which someone has to answer questions
2. _____	=	not expected to change or be in any danger
3. _____	=	something that is very surprising, usually in a bad way
4. _____	=	have a final result you did not expect
5. _____	=	the number of points someone gets on a test or in a game

Building on the Vocabulary

> **Word Grammar: Phrasal Verbs**
>
> *Deal with* is a **phrasal verb**. So are *end up* and *give up*. Phrasal verbs have two parts: a verb (such as *make, get,* or *turn*) and a particle (such as *up, out,* or *off*).
>
> The meaning of the phrasal verb is different from the meanings of its two parts. For example, *give up* means you stop trying to do something, usually because you believe you cannot succeed. That is very different from giving something to someone.
>
> Phrasal verbs, like other verbs, can have more than one meaning. Look for them in your dictionary at the end of the entry for the verb.

Circle the correct phrasal verb to complete the sentence.

1. You can never be sure which horse will (figure out / end up) winning the race. You have to wait until they finish to find out.

2. My brothers sometimes get angry when they talk about the family business. Their discussions sometimes (turn into / deal with) fights.

3. We need help with this problem. We can't (end up / figure out) what to do.

4. Don't worry. I'm sure everything will (turn out / figure out) well in the end.

5. The police have to (deal with / give up) difficult people all the time.

6. I failed the driving test on my first try, but I'll try again. I won't (turn into / give up).

DEVELOPING YOUR READING SKILLS

Topics of Paragraphs

Look at the list of paragraph topics from "Life is Full of Surprises." Find the paragraph on each topic in the reading. Write the paragraph number (1–7).

a. Mahmoud's study of English   Paragraph _____

b. Mahmoud's life today   Paragraph _____

c. things Mahmoud never expected   Paragraph __1__

d. how the revolution changed Mahmoud's life   Paragraph _____

e. how an exam changed Mahmoud's life   Paragraph _____

f. reaching a goal   Paragraph _____

g. a job offer in Tehran   Paragraph _____

Main Ideas

A. What is the main idea of the reading? Check ☑ your answer.

- ☐ 1. Mahmoud Arani grew up in Iran, but now he lives with his family in the United States.

- ☐ 2. Some changes happened in Mahmoud Arani's life that were disappointing and even shocking.

- ☐ 3. Mahmoud Arani had to deal with some big changes in his life, but he managed to do that well.

B. What is the main idea of paragraph 4 in the reading? Check ☑ your answer.

- ☐ 1. Mahmoud decided that he wanted to teach in New York, not in Tehran.

- ☐ 2. Mahmoud was happy to have a teaching job waiting for him at a university in Tehran.

- ☐ 3. Mahmoud made officials at the university in Tehran angry by going back to New York.

Understanding Cause and Effect

Complete the following sentences with *because* using information from "Life Is Full of Surprises."

1. Mahmoud's grade on the exam surprised his teachers because _____

_____.

2. Mahmoud went to the United States because _____

_____.

3. As an international student, Mahmoud was unusual because

_____.

4. Mahmoud lost the chance to teach in Tehran because

_____

_____.

> **Reading Tip:** When you read, look for the writer's **point of view**, or what the writer thinks about the topic. What does the exclamation point (!) at the end of paragraph 3 tell you about the writer's point of view?

CRITICAL THINKING

Discussion

Talk with your class about these questions.

1. What were two big surprises in Mahmoud's life? How did Mahmoud deal with each of these surprises? Underline the parts of the reading that help you answer the question. What can you infer from Mahmoud's words and actions about the kind of person he is?

2. In paragraph 7, when Mahmoud says that "life is full of surprises," what does he mean? Do you share his point of view? Are surprises a good thing in life? Why or why not?

3. Mahmoud says that he could go to medical school now (paragraph 7). Is he going to become a doctor? Underline the part of the reading that supports your answer. What does he mean when he says "if I had the patience"? Why do you think he says this?

4. Why do you think Mahmoud chose to become a teacher? What information in the reading helps you answer this question? What are some other reasons that people become teachers? Would you like to teach? Would you like to teach English?

> **Critical Thinking Tip:** Sometimes a reading does not say something openly. We need to figure it out for ourselves. We use the information the writer gives us to **infer**, or make guesses, about what the writer does not say.

WRITING

A. Use the Target Vocabulary: Choose five target words or phrases from the chart on pages 52–53. On a piece of paper, use each word or phrase in a sentence. Then find a partner. Read each other's sentences.

B. Practice Writing: Choose one of these topics and write a short paragraph about it. Then find a partner and read each other's paragraphs.

1. Describe a time in your life when you set a goal and didn't give up. What were you trying to do? What made it hard? How did you reach your goal?

2. Think back to an earlier stage in your life. Write about a time when you wanted something very much. Did you get what you wanted, or were you disappointed? What did this experience mean to you? Did it change you in any way? Explain.

> **Writing Tip:** Make sure you understand the topic you choose before you begin writing your paragraph. After you write, read the questions again. Does your paragraph answer them?

CHAPTER 6

Arunaa on her wedding day

"It Was Love, So Strong and So Real"

LEARNING OUTCOME

❯ Learn about an international love story

GETTING READY TO READ

Talk about these questions with a partner.

1. You're going to read a love story. It's about two people from opposite sides of the world. What do you think might be difficult for this couple?

2. How important is it for married people to have things in common[1] with each other? Choose a number between 1 (extremely important) and 4 (not important at all). Explain your answer.

[1] *have things in common = share the same experiences, opinions, family background, etc.*

Read to Find Out: How did Arunaa's life change?

Look at the words and definitions next to the reading. Then read without stopping.

"It Was Love, So Strong and So Real"

1   Arunaa was in her last year of college near her home in Malaysia. It was the first day of a new course, and she was in class. "Suddenly," she says, "I had this **awful** feeling of being watched." She looked across the room and found that someone was **staring** at her—an exchange student[1] from Europe. He continued looking at her all through the class. He did it the next day, too, and the next. Finally, she told herself, "Enough! I'm going to talk to him. That will stop him." So she went and sat down next to him. She **discovered** that his name was Hervé and he was French. "As soon as we started talking, it was magic[2] and he was perfect."

2   Arunaa and Hervé fell in love, but after a few months, he had to return to France. Soon after that, Arunaa graduated and **faced** the biggest decision of her life. Hervé wanted her to come to Paris: Should she go, or should she try to forget him?

3   Arunaa remembers, "My parents were in **total** shock, but the best thing was that they never said no. It was always my choice and my **responsibility**. This is what they always taught me, to make my own decisions."

4   It was hard for Arunaa to think of leaving family, friends, and home. Living in France would be a **challenge**, too. **For one thing**, she did not speak French. "And it was difficult for me," she says, "because I wasn't really sure what to expect. When I met Hervé, he was a student, and almost like a tourist.[3] He was happy in Malaysia and he felt **comfortable** there, but that wasn't real life for him. I **was about to** meet another Hervé, whom I didn't know—the Hervé who was **no longer** a student but a man with a serious job, and a Frenchman in his own country."

5   Arunaa decided to go. "I had to take the chance.[4] **Although** there were many **differences** between us, we were so much **alike**! I knew that he was the one for me." For Arunaa and Hervé, it was the right decision, and now they are happily married.

6   **Marriage** is not easy, and it's even harder when two people have to deal with differences in language, religion, and culture. Arunaa says, "The cultural differences were enormous.[5] I come from an Islamic country, although my family is Christian, and many things in France shocked me." The hardest thing, she says, is to understand the way that French people think.

[1] *exchange student* = someone who studies for a while at a foreign university

[2] *it was magic* = it was surprising, exciting, wonderful

[3] *tourist* = someone who is traveling for fun

[4] *take the chance* = do something that may be dangerous

[5] *enormous* = very, very big

7 Smaller differences in their everyday life caused problems, too. Arunaa laughs, "We are like night and day! I eat rice three times a day, and I don't wear shoes in the house. Also, I want to take care of my husband, like my mother and her mother before her, but that makes Hervé uncomfortable." Even with all the challenges, after 13 years and one child together, they are still very much in love.

Quick Comprehension Check

A. Read these sentences. Circle T (true) or F (false). On the line, write the number of the paragraph with the answer.

1. Arunaa is from Malaysia.   T   F   _____
2. She met Hervé when she was a college student in France.   T   F   _____
3. She was in a hurry to get away from home.   T   F   _____
4. Arunaa's parents told her not to leave home.   T   F   _____
5. Arunaa moved to France to be with Hervé.   T   F   _____
6. It was hard for Arunaa to get used to many things in her new life.   T   F   _____

B. Work with your class. Share your answers from part A. Go back to the reading to find the reason why a sentence is true or false. Correct the false sentences.

EXPLORING VOCABULARY

Thinking about the Target Vocabulary

A. Look at the chart with the target vocabulary. Four nouns are missing. Scan the reading to find them. Add them to the correct places in the chart. Write the singular form of any plural noun.

¶	Nouns	Verbs	Adjectives	Other
1			awful	
		stare		
		discover		
2		face		
3			total	
4				

¶	Nouns	Verbs	Adjectives	Other
				for one thing
			comfortable	
		be about to		
				no longer
5				although
		alike		
6				

B. Which words and phrases are new to you? Circle them in the chart. Then find them in the reading. Look at the context. Can you guess the meaning?

Using the Target Vocabulary

A. These sentences are about the reading. What is the meaning of each **boldfaced** word or phrase? Circle a, b, or c.

1. One day in class, Arunaa had an **awful** feeling. She didn't like it. *Awful* means

   a. lonely. b. terrible. c. natural.

2. Arunaa saw someone new across the room. He was **staring at** her. *Stare at someone* means

   a. speak to them. b. point a finger at them. c. keep looking at them.

3. By talking to him, she **discovered** that he was French. *Discover* means

   a. find out. b. mention. c. accept.

4. Arunaa had to **face** a big decision. *Face* means

   a. turn into. b. deal with. c. give up.

5. Arunaa says that the idea of her going to France was a big surprise to her parents. They were "in **total** shock." *Total* means

   a. local. b. complete. c. natural.

6. Arunaa worried about living in France. She thought that it would be a **challenge** for her. A challenge is

   a. something hard to do. b. a good choice. c. the only thing available.

7. Hervé felt **comfortable** in Malaysia. It was good to be there. If you are comfortable, you are

   a. stressed.   b. bored.   c. feeling fine.

8. When Arunaa was on her way to France, she knew she **was about to** "meet another Hervé." When you are about to do something, you are going to do it

   a. alone.   b. very soon.   c. suddenly.

9. **Although** there were many differences between Arunaa and Hervé, they were the same in important ways. Use *although* to introduce the first part of a sentence when the second part

   a. gives a reason.   b. repeats the first part.   c. seems surprising.

10. Arunaa says they are different in some ways but **alike** in others. *Alike* means

   a. the same or nearly the same.   b. disappointed or unhappy   c. safe or secure.

Vocabulary Tip: Learn the other words in the same word family as *comfortable*. *Comfort* can be a noun or a verb. The opposite of *comfortable* is *uncomfortable*.

Writing Tip: Use *although*, like *but*, to show a contrast. Look at how the two words are used differently: *Although it was cold, he didn't wear a coat.* = *It was cold, but he didn't wear a coat.*

B. These sentences use the target words and phrases **in new contexts**. Complete them with the words and phrases in the box.

alike	are about to	challenge	discovered	stare
although	awful	comfortable	face	total

1. We looked out the window and _____ that it was snowing. What a surprise!

2. It's natural to want to look at other people, but I don't think it's polite to _____ at them.

3. _____ he's not tall, he's a good basketball player.

4. I like to do things that test my skills and abilities. I enjoy a _____.

5. Chris and Pat are too different to be good roommates for each other. They are _____ opposites.

6. You can't run away from this problem. You have to _____ it.

7. I'll have to call you back. I'm at the airport, standing in line, and we _____ get on our plane.

8. I was very _____ in bed, and so I didn't want to get up.

9. She and her sister look _____, but they dress very

   differently.

10. I hated the movie. I thought it was _____.

C. Read each definition and look at the paragraph number. Look back at the reading on pages 60–61 to find the **boldfaced** word or phrase to match the definition. Copy it in the chart.

Definition	Paragraph	Target Word or Phrase
1. something you have to do or take care of	3	
2. a phrase used to introduce the first of several reasons	4	
3. not now, not anymore	4	
4. ways that two people or things are not like each other	5	
5. the relationship of two married people	6	

Building on the Vocabulary

Word Grammar: Count Nouns and Noncount Nouns

Count nouns have singular and plural forms: *one pen, two pens; a man, several men.*

Noncount nouns (or **uncountable nouns**) have only one form: *air, water, music.*
Do not use *a, an,* or a number with a noncount noun.
When a noncount noun is the subject of a verb, use a singular verb.

Some nouns can be both a count and a noncount noun. Each one has a different meaning. Look at these examples.

Count Nouns	Noncount Nouns
I called you three **times** and left three messages.	How much **time** do we have before class?
How many different **varieties** of breakfast cereal does the supermarket sell?	"**Variety** is the spice of life" means that doing different things is what makes life interesting.

Look up *time* in your dictionary to see how your dictionary marks nouns as countable or uncountable. For example, in Longman dictionaries for learners of English, you will see nouns marked [C] and [U].

Look at the **boldfaced** nouns. Are they countable? Circle *count* or *noncount*. Check your answers in your dictionary.

1. What are the **differences** between the two cases?   count   noncount

2. We can go either way. It doesn't make much **difference**.   count   noncount

3. There's a five-hour time **difference** between Rome and New York.   count   noncount

4. Before getting their son a pet, they talked about his **responsibilities** as a pet owner.   count   noncount

5. Mike has a strong sense of **responsibility** for his younger brothers.   count   noncount

6. The store accepted **responsibility** for the mistake and gave me my money back.   count   noncount

DEVELOPING YOUR READING SKILLS

Identifying Paragraph Topics

What is each paragraph in the reading about? Write the topics of the paragraphs.

1. Paragraph 1: *how Arunaa and Hervé met*

2. Paragraph 2: _____

3. Paragraph 3: _____

4. Paragraph 4: _____

5. Paragraph 5: _____

6. Paragraph 6: _____

7. Paragraph 7: _____

> **Reading Tip:**
> By identifying the topic of each paragraph, you can make a map in your mind of how the information in the reading is organized.

Reading for Details

Are these statements about the reading true or false? If the reading doesn't give the information, check (✓) *It doesn't say.*

	True	False	It doesn't say.
1. Arunaa met Hervé in a college classroom in Malaysia.			
2. Hervé left before Arunaa graduated.			
3. Arunaa expected him to come back.			

	True	False	It doesn't say.
4. Arunaa's parents told her not to go to France.			
5. Hervé expected things to be easy for Arunaa in France.			
6. Arunaa says her biggest challenge was religious differences.			
7. In France, Arunaa still eats rice three times a day.			
8. Arunaa can speak French well now.			

Making Inferences

Reading Between the Lines

Reading between the lines means figuring out some meaning that is hidden or not given openly. Readers have to make **inferences**—guesses that they base on the information the writer gives and on what they already know.

Make inferences. Answer these questions with your own opinions.

1. Why was Hervé staring at Arunaa in class?

   _____.

2. Why were Arunaa's parents in shock?

   _____.

3. What worried Arunaa most when she thought about going to France?

   _____.

4. Why doesn't Arunaa wear shoes in the house?

   _____.

CRITICAL THINKING

Discussion

Talk about these questions in a small group.

1. The phrase *love at first sight* is used to describe a love that someone feels from the first time they meet someone. Do you think Arunaa would say that she fell in love at first sight? Underline information in the reading that supports your opinion. Explain your answer.

2. Arunaa wondered if she should go to France or try to forget Hervé. What reasons for and against going to France can you find in the reading?

Complete the first row of the chart. Then add any other reasons your group can think of in the bottom row. Check (✔) the reasons that *you* think are most important to consider.

	Reasons to Go	Reasons Not to Go
From the text		
Your ideas		

3. How did Arunaa's parents feel about the idea of Arunaa going to join Hervé in France? Underline information in the reading that supports your answer. What did Arunaa's parents tell her? Would you have done the same if it were your daughter? Explain.

4. What was Arunaa's biggest challenge in France? Underline the part of the reading where you find the answer. What do you think made this hard for Arunaa?

5. Look at paragraph 7 and find the phrase Arunaa uses to describe herself and Hervé. What does this phrase mean? What examples does she give to support it? What can you infer about Hervé?

6. List the changes that moving to France made in Arunaa's life. Did she manage to deal with them well? Explain your answer. If you have had the experience of moving to another country, describe some changes in your life. How does your experience compare with Arunaa's?

> **Critical Thinking Tip:** A chart with two columns is called a T-chart. Use this kind of graphic organizer to compare and contrast information side-by-side.

WRITING

A. Use the Target Vocabulary: Choose five target words or phrases from the list on pages 61–62. On a piece of paper, use each word or phrase in a sentence. Underline the target vocabulary. Then find a partner and read each other's sentences.

B. Practice Writing: Choose one of these topics and write a short paragraph about it. Then find a partner and read each other's paragraphs.

1. Do you believe in love at first sight? Write a paragraph to answer the question. You can begin: *I (believe/don't believe) in love at first sight because...*

2. When did you face a big decision in your life? What did you decide? How did you feel about it then? How do you feel about it now?

> **Writing Tip:** You may not really know at first if you agree or disagree with an idea. Before you write, try using a T-chart to list reasons for and against. This can help make your ideas clearer.

CHAPTER 7

To Live as an Artist

Czechoslovakia in 1981

LEARNING OUTCOME

› Learn about someone who had to leave his country

GETTING READY TO READ

Talk about these questions in a small group.

1. Some people leave their country because they have to. What are some reasons why some people *must* leave?

2. Vitek Kruta was born in communist[1] Czechoslovakia.[2] Look at the countries in this list. Which ones have, or used to have, a communist government? Check ☑ your answers.

	In the Past	Now	Never
a. Russia	☐	☐	☐
b. China	☐	☐	☐
c. Japan	☐	☐	☐
d. Spain	☐	☐	☐
e. Cuba	☐	☐	☐

[1] *communist* = having government control of all land, factories, food production, schools, etc.

[2] *Czechoslovakia*— In 1993, it became two countries, the Czech Republic and Slovakia.

READING

Read to Find Out: What are the biggest changes Vitek has experienced in his life?

Look at the pictures, words, and definitions next to the reading. Then read without stopping.

To Live as an Artist

1 In 1981, the artist Vitek Kruta **escaped** from his country. He left with just one little bag. "One little bag with basic things like a toothbrush and underwear," he remembers. He was nineteen years old at the time.

2 Vitek's home was in Prague, Czechoslovakia. He loved his country, but he could not stay there because the communist government wanted to put him in jail.[1] "The government wanted total **control** of all art and music," he explains. "We had to have art shows in secret. My kind of painting was **against the law**. The rock music that my band played was against the law. There was no future for me there." So Vitek escaped to Germany. The rest of his family was still in Prague, and after he left, the police made a lot of trouble for his father.

3 In Germany, Vitek first had to learn the language. He spoke Czech and Russian but not German, so he spent eight months taking **lessons** at a language school. Vitek remembers that it was easy for him to understand and read German, but he could not speak it. Then one night, he had a dream. In his dream, he was skiing[2] in the mountains. He met another skier and started talking with him—in German! The following day, he discovered that he could speak much better.

4 Next, Vitek **got back to** his studies in art. He learned to restore[3] old buildings such as churches and castles.[4] He spent ten years doing this kind of work, and then he faced another big change in his life: He got a job offer in the United States. Vitek knew **hardly** any English, but he did not let that stop him. **After all**, he had **a great deal** of experience learning new languages. So he and his wife, Lucie, decided to make the move.

5 Today, Vitek is a painter, an architect,[5] and much more. He is a man with a lot of **energy**. He works in his studio,[6] he teaches art classes, and he helps **manage** an art school.

6 Vitek also likes to get people with different **talents** and abilities together to do big art **projects**. Sometimes he has a group work on restoring a building. Sometimes they **cover** a room with murals (large pictures painted on the walls). Vitek likes to do projects in public places—at schools or in city buildings or in churches—so that anyone can see and enjoy them. He says that projects like these "bring art back to the people."

[1] *jail* = a room or building where the police can hold someone

[2] *skiing*

[3] *restore* = make like new again

[4] *a castle*

[5] *architect* = a person whose job is planning new buildings

[6] *studio* = the workplace of an artist

7   Vitek believes that art plays an important **role** in the world. Art lets
     people be creative,[7] and the world needs creative people. Vitek explains,
     "If we are not free to be creative—and I'm talking about scientists and
     mathematicians, too, not just artists—then human beings can only
     copy the past. We cannot move **forward**."

[7] *creative* = good at thinking of and making new things

Quick Comprehension Check

A. Read these sentences. Circle T (true) or F (false). On the line, write the
number of the paragraph with the answer.

1.	Vitek grew up in communist Czechoslovakia.	T	F	____
2.	At age nineteen, he went to jail.	T	F	____
3.	He learned German in Germany.	T	F	____
4.	Now he lives and works in the United States.	T	F	____
5.	He is uncomfortable sharing his art with other people.	T	F	____
6.	Vitek thinks that no one really needs art, but it's fun.	T	F	____

B. Work with your class. Share your answers from part A. Go back to the
reading to find the reason why a sentence is true or false. Correct the false
sentences.

EXPLORING VOCABULARY

Thinking about the Target Vocabulary

A. Look at the chart with the target vocabulary. Four verbs are missing. Scan
the reading to find them. Add them to the correct places in the chart. Write
the base form of each verb.

¶	Nouns	Verbs	Adjectives	Other
1				
2	control			
				against the law
3	lesson			
4				
				hardly
				after all

¶	Nouns	Verbs	Adjectives	Other
				a great deal
5	energy			
6	talent			
	project			
7	role			
				forward

B. Which words and phrases are new to you? Circle them in the chart. Then find them in the reading. Look at the context. Can you guess the meaning?

Using the Target Vocabulary

A. These sentences are **about the reading**. Complete them with the target words and phrases in the box.

after all	control	escaped	hardly	projects
a great deal	cover	forward	manage	role

1. In 1981, people were not free to leave Czechoslovakia when they wanted to, so Vitek had to leave secretly. He _____.

2. Artists and musicians in Czechoslovakia were not free to do what they wanted. The government wanted _____ of all art and music.

3. Vitek knew almost no English before moving to the United States. He knew _____ any English.

4. Vitek knew very little English, but he still decided to move to the United States. Perhaps that's not surprising. _____, he'd had a lot of practice learning new languages. He knew he could do it again.

> **Vocabulary Tip:**
> Use *after all* to introduce a fact that someone should remember or consider, one that helps to explain the information that came before.

5. Vitek had already learned Russian and German (and of course Czech, his first language), so he had _____ of experience as a language learner.

6. Today Vitek is one of the decision-makers for an art school. He helps _____ the school.

7. Vitek sometimes paints murals. A mural is a large painting that is painted on a wall. It can _____ a whole wall.

8. Vitek likes to do big art _____ in public places, where anyone can enter. These are carefully planned pieces of work that often take a long time.

9. Vitek believes that art has an important job to do in the world. He thinks art should play a big _____ in our lives.

10. He also believes that human beings shouldn't stay as we are now. We should keep learning and move _____ with new ideas to make the world a better place.

B. These sentences use the target words and phrases **in new contexts**. Complete them with the words and phrases in the box.

after all	control	escape	hardly	projects
a great deal	covered	forward	manages	role

1. Olivia owns and _____ the company. Ten people work for her.

2. The plan for building the new school cannot go _____ without more money.

3. Snow fell during the night. It completely _____ everything outdoors.

4. On an icy road, a driver can lose _____ of his or her car.

5. The fifth grade students spent weeks working on their science _____.

6. My grandfather is 92, but he continues to play a big _____ in running the family business.

7. The message was very short. It _____ said anything at all.

8. Randy knows a lot about taxes. He knows _____ more than I do.

9. The cat has to stay inside, so please close the door, or she might _____.

Writing Tip: You can also use *a great deal + of + noncount noun*: *a great deal of responsibility (control, energy, talent)*.

10. Ann isn't worried about having the baby because she knows what to expect. _____, this will be her third child.

C. Read the sentences. Guess the meaning of the **boldfaced** target words and phrases from the context. Match them with their definitions.

a. His parents discovered his musical **talent** when he was very young.
b. She wants to learn to fly a plane, so she's taking flying **lessons**.
c. I took a short break and then **got back to** work.
d. Children can't drive. It's **against the law**.
e. The children were full of **energy**, and they played for hours in the park.

Target Word or Phrase	Definition
1. _____	= a time when someone works with a teacher to learn a skill
2. _____	= a natural ability to do something well
3. _____	= the power of body and mind that lets you be active and do things
4. _____	= returned to (something you were doing)
5. _____	= in disagreement with or opposed to the rules set by the government

Building on the Vocabulary

> **Word Grammar: *Hard* and *Hardly***
>
> The adverbs *hardly* and *hard* are very different in meaning.
>
> *It was raining hard.* = The rain was coming down with a lot of force.
>
> *In the rain, I could hardly see to drive.* = I could almost not see well enough to drive.
>
> Here are two ways to use *hardly* in sentences.
>
> Use *hardly* + a verb. It has a negative meaning ("almost not"). Do not use it with another negative word:
>
> *I hardly never see her.*
>
> Use *hardly* + *any* + a plural or noncount noun. It means "almost none."
>
> We had *hardly any* problems.
>
> There is *hardly any* time left.

Rewrite these sentences using *hardly*.

1. I almost can't hear you.

   _____

2. The baby almost never cries.

   _____

3. They almost never speak in class.

   _____

4. There were almost no other people at the movie.

   _____

5. I have almost no free time.

   _____

DEVELOPING YOUR READING SKILLS

Understanding Text Features

> **Text Features: Footnotes, Notes in the Margin, and Tip Boxes**
>
> In this book, you will see **footnotes** and notes in the **margin**. You will see an asterisk (*) or a superscript number after a word (like [2]) when there is a footnote about it at the bottom of the page or a note about it in the right margin of the reading. The footnotes add extra information. Notes in the margin give definitions and illustrations of words and phrases. Also in the margin are **tip boxes** that give useful information about reading, vocabulary, critical thinking, and writing.

Answer the questions.

1. Where in this chapter do you find a footnote about Czechoslovakia? On page

   _____

2. How many notes in the margin are there for the reading "To Live as an

   Artist"? _____

3. What words in the reading have illustrations in the margin?

   _____ and _____

4. How many tip boxes do you find in this chapter? _____

Scanning

Read these questions about "To Live as an Artist." Scan the reading and write your answers. If you use a sentence or phrase from the reading, copy it carefully and put quotation marks around it.

> **Reading Tip:** When you read—and especially when you scan—don't say the words in your mind or move your lips. That will slow you down.

   1. In what city did Vitek Kruta grow up? _____

   2. When did he escape from Czechoslovakia? _____

   3. What did he take with him?

      _____

   4. Where did he go first? _____

   5. How long did he live there? _____

   6. Where does he live now? _____

   7. What languages does he know now?

      _____

   8. What are three types of work Vitek does?

      _____

Making Inferences

To answer these questions, you need to make inferences. Tell what you think is true, based on information in the reading. Give the reasons for your answers.

1. Did Vitek ask the government to let him leave Czechoslovakia?

   _____

   _____

2. Is Vitek good at dealing with changes in his life?

_____

_____

3. Is Vitek living the life he dreamed of when he was a young man?

_____

_____

CRITICAL THINKING

Discussion

Talk about these questions in a small group.

1. The title of Unit 2 is "Life Changes." Why is Vitek's story in this unit? What changes does the reading discuss? In what ways is Vitek's story like Mahmoud's (in Chapter 5) or Arunaa's (in Chapter 6)?

2. Read again about Vitek's dream (paragraph 3). What changed for him after this dream? You are an experienced language learner: Why do you think that happened?

3. The writer calls Vitek "a man with a lot of energy" (paragraph 5). How does the writer support that statement? Do you agree with the writer's opinion?

4. Underline the parts of the reading that explain Vitek's ideas about art in public places. Do you agree with him? Can you give any examples of art in public places where you live or have lived in the past? Does art play a role in your own life? Explain.

5. The last words of the reading are "move forward." What do they mean in this context? In Vitek's opinion, what helps us to move forward? Do you share his point of view? Explain.

> **Critical Thinking Tip:** When a writer states an opinion, look to see how the writer supports that opinion. What facts, examples, or other details does the writer give to try to get you to agree?

WRITING

A. Use the Target Vocabulary: Choose five target words or phrases from the list on pages 70–71. On a piece of paper, use each word or phrase in a sentence. Underline the target vocabulary. Then find a partner and read each other's sentences.

B. Practice Writing. Choose one of these topics and write a short paragraph about it. Then find a partner and read each other's paragraphs.

1. Do you know someone who has a special talent? Describe the person and what he or she can do that is special.

2. Do you know someone who is full of energy? What does this person do that shows how much energy he or she has?

> **Writing Tip:** Begin your paragraph with a sentence that gives the main idea of your paragraph. After you write, make sure all your sentences support that main idea.

CHAPTER 8

An Amazing Woman

Ruth Simmons

LEARNING OUTCOME

> Learn how education changed someone's life

GETTING READY TO READ

Talk about this question in a small group.

You are going to read about big changes in Ruth Simmons's life. You will also read about changes in the United States during the last sixty years. Think about your country sixty years ago. What is one thing that is now very different? Complete this sentence:

Sixty years ago in my country, _____

but now _____.

Read to Find Out: What does Ruth Simmons believe in?

Look at the words and definitions next to the reading. Then read without stopping.

An Amazing Woman

1   Ruth Simmons was born into a very poor family, but she grew up to become the president of a famous university. How did she do it? Hers is an **amazing** story.

2   The story begins on a farm in Grapeland, Texas, in 1945, the year that Ruth was born. Her parents were farmworkers, and she was the youngest of their twelve children. They could not give their children many things, and Ruth never had any toys to play with. For Christmas, she did not receive any presents at all **except** a shoebox with an apple, an orange, and some nuts. However, in Grapeland, Ruth was not really **aware** of being poor. No one else had much, either. Then the family moved into the city, to Houston, where people had more money and being poor was much harder for Ruth. In school, other children laughed at the way she spoke and dressed.

3   Ruth's mother kept the family together. She had no education, "but she was very **wise**," Ruth remembers. "She taught us about the real **value** of being a human being, what **mattered** and what didn't matter." Ruth's mother did not have big dreams. She just wanted to see her children grow up. This was not a simple wish. At that time, there was segregation[1] in the United States, and life was dangerous for African-Americans, especially in the South.[2] Ruth remembers living in **fear**. "If you looked at someone the wrong way, you could be killed."

4   At age five, Ruth fell in love with school. She was lucky to have some excellent teachers. No one in Ruth's family had much education, but her teachers **encouraged** her to go to college. They gave her money and even a coat to wear. Ruth knew that college was going to be difficult, but she was **brave** enough to give it a try.

5   At first, Ruth studied theater,[3] but what kind of **career** in theater could a young African-American woman hope for? She says, "Remember, I grew up in the South; I couldn't even go to theaters." So she studied languages **instead**. Later, she married, had two children, began a teaching career, and became a college administrator.[4] Soon, people began to **notice** her and respect her abilities.

[1] *segregation* = making African-Americans go to different schools, restaurants, etc., from people of other races

[2] *the South* = the southern U.S. states where African-Americans were held as slaves from the 1600s until 1863

[3] *theater* = (a) reading, writing, and acting in plays; (b) a place where you see a movie or a play

[4] *an administrator* = a manager in the government, a school, a business, etc.

6   In 1995, Ruth became president of Smith College, a famous U.S. college for women. Ruth was the first African-American to **lead** such a famous college. Suddenly, her story was on TV and in newspapers all over the country. Six years later, she accepted another challenge. She became the president of Brown University and was the first woman in that role.

7   Ruth **believes in** the **power** of education. She once said, "Learning can be the same for a poor farm kid like me as it is for the richest child in the country. It's all about cultivating one's mind,[5] and anybody can do that. So it doesn't matter what color your skin is, it doesn't matter how much money your father has, it doesn't matter what kind of house you live in. Every learner can experience the same thing." As Ruth Simmons will tell you, education can change your life.

[5] *cultivating one's mind* = developing your thinking skills

President Simmons's words come from "Poised for the Presidency" by Judith Gingerich and Sarah Curran Barrett, Smith Alumnae Quarterly, Winter 1995/96. The final quotation has been simplified.

Quick Comprehension Check

A. Read these sentences. Circle T (true) or F (false). On the line, write the number of the paragraph with the answer.

1. Ruth Simmons became the president of a famous university.   T   F   ____

2. She grew up in a very poor family.   T   F   ____

3. She grew up during a dangerous time for African-Americans.   T   F   ____

4. Ruth's mother always expected Ruth to become famous.   T   F   ____

5. Ruth always wanted a career as a college president.   T   F   ____

6. Ruth's message is that education can change any person's life.   T   F   ____

B. Work with your class. Share your answers from part A. Go back to the reading to find the reason why a sentence is true or false. Correct the false sentences.

EXPLORING VOCABULARY

Thinking about the Target Vocabulary

A. Look at the chart with the target vocabulary. Five verbs and four adjectives are missing. Scan the reading to find them. Add them to the correct places in the chart. Write the base form of each verb.

¶	Nouns	Verbs	Adjectives	Other
1				
2				except
3				
	value			
	fear			
4				
5	career			
				instead
6				
7				
	power			

B. Which words are new to you? Circle them in the chart. Then find the words in the reading. Look at the context. Can you guess the meaning?

Using the Target Vocabulary

A. These sentences are **about the reading**. What is the meaning of each **boldfaced** word? Circle a, b, or c.

1. Ruth Simmons has had a very unusual life. Her life story is **amazing**. *Amazing* means
   - a. common and expected.
   - b. surprising and wonderful.
   - c. slow and boring.

2. Ruth's family was like all the families in Grapeland, so she wasn't **aware of** being poor. If you are aware of something, you

    a. are proud of it.   b. are excited about it.   c. know about it.

Vocabulary Tip: *Aware* is usually followed by *of* + noun or *that* + subject + verb: *He's aware of the danger. He's aware that it is dangerous.*

3. Although she had no education, Ruth's mother was very **wise**. People went to her for advice. *Wise* means

    a. able to make good decisions.   b. afraid of many things.   c. sad and lonely.

4. Ruth's mother taught her children the true **value** of things in life. The value of a thing is

    a. where it comes from.   b. its history.   c. how much it's worth.

5. Ruth learned from her mother what to care about—what does and does not **matter** in life. The things that matter are

    a. average.   b. popular.   c. important.

6. Ruth and many other African-Americans lived in **fear** of being killed. *Lived in fear* means they

    a. were always afraid.   b. were comfortable.   c. stayed in a specific area.

7. Ruth was nervous about college. She had to be **brave** to try it. *Brave* means

    a. ready to face danger.   b. too afraid to do something.   c. bored or tired.

8. In college, Ruth studied theater at first. Then she changed her mind and studied languages **instead**. *Instead* means

    a. no longer.   b. in place of something else.   c. in general.

9. People **noticed** Ruth's abilities and respected her work. *Notice* means

    a. produce or make.   b. become aware of.   c. laugh at.

10. Ruth grew up to **lead** a famous U.S. university. *Lead* means

    a. study or learn.   b. discover or find out.   c. show others what to do.

B. These sentences use the target words **in new contexts**. Complete them with the words in the box.

amazing	brave	instead	matter	value
aware	fear	lead	notice	wise

1. You don't have to rush. It doesn't _____ if we get there late.

2. Mike didn't join the army. _____, he went to Hollywood to become an actor.

3. People expect firefighters to be _____ because they face danger in their work.

4. I didn't know that. I wasn't _____ of the problem. Please explain it to me.

5. The cat didn't _____ the bird until it began to sing.

6. We all understand the _____ of a good education.

7. People often go to him for advice. He's a very _____ man.

8. You can speak six languages? That's _____!

9. Ali knew the way to go and we didn't, so I said, "You _____, please, and we'll follow."

10. Many people are afraid to fly. Many others have a _____ of public speaking.

Writing Tip: Use the adverb *instead* at the beginning or the end of a sentence: *He went to Hollywood instead.* You can also use *instead* + *of* + noun: *Mike became an actor instead of a soldier.*

C. Read the sentences. Guess the meaning of the **boldfaced** target words from the context. Match them with their definitions.

   a. I **encourage** her to call us if she has any problem.
   b. The president has the **power** and the responsibility to lead the country.
   c. Peter had a long **career** as a researcher.
   d. Everyone is here today **except** Jamal. He's sick.
   e. I **believe in** the Golden Rule: *Treat other people the way you would like them to treat you.*

Target Word or Phrase	Definition
1. _____	= besides, not including
2. _____	= think something is right and good
3. _____	= the ability to control people and events
4. _____	= the years of someone's life spent working in a profession
5. _____	= say or do things to help a person feel ready to try something

Building on the Vocabulary

Word Grammar: Some Meanings and Uses of *Value*

Value has several meanings. It can be a count noun, a noncount noun, or a verb. Read the definitions below, and see your dictionary for more information.

value n. [U] the importance or usefulness of something

values n. [plural] a person's ideas about what is right and wrong and what is important in life

value v. think that (something) is important

Complete these sentences with **value** or **values**.

1. I _____ her as a friend.

2. He understands the _____ of hard work.

3. We are a lot alike. We share the same _____.

DEVELOPING YOUR READING SKILLS

Reading for Details

Are these statements about the reading true or false? If the reading doesn't give the information, check (✓) **It doesn't say.**

	True	False	It doesn't say.
1. Ruth Simmons was born in the United States.			
2. She had younger brothers and sisters.			
3. Even as a child, she was aware of the dangers for African-Americans.			
4. She enjoyed school and did well there.			
5. Ruth's parents encouraged her to go to college.			
6. Her teachers helped her go to college.			
7. She felt that planning a career in theater was a wise idea for her.			
8. She became the first woman to lead a famous U.S. college.			

Understanding Cause and Effect

Complete the following sentences with *because* using information from "An Amazing Woman."

Reading Tip:
Sometimes a writer does not state the reason for something. You need to read between the lines to figure out the cause.

1. As a child, Ruth was not aware of how poor her family was because

   _____.

2. Ruth's mother did not have big dreams for her children's futures because

   _____.

3. Ruth changed her mind about studying theater in college because

   _____.

4. Ruth believes that learning can be the same for both rich and poor children

   because _____.

Summarizing

Critical Thinking Tip:
Summarizing a reading makes you think about which ideas are most important and figure out how to put them into writing. It helps you understand and remember what you read.

Write a summary of "An Amazing Woman." Write it as a paragraph. Include the answers to these questions:

- Who is Ruth Simmons?
- What is unusual about her life story?
- What does she believe in?

You can begin:

> Ruth Simmons is an African-American woman who became the president of Brown University in the United States. She grew up . . .

CRITICAL THINKING

Discussion

Talk about these questions in a small group.

1. The title of the reading is "An Amazing Woman." Do you think it is a good title for Ruth Simmons's life story? Use information from the reading to explain your answer.

2. Ruth is quoted in paragraph 3 as saying, "If you looked at someone the wrong way, you could be killed." Who is "you" in this sentence? What does she mean by "looked at someone the wrong way?" Are there places where this still true? Explain your answer.

3. In paragraph 5, the writer quotes Ruth: "Remember, I grew up in the South; I couldn't even *go* to theaters." What does Ruth mean? What is the purpose of this sentence in the paragraph?

4. Ruth has strong ideas about what's right and what's wrong and what is most important in life. Where did she learn these values? Underline the parts of the reading that support your answer. How do you think most people learn their values?

5. In Unit 2, you read about changes in people's lives that were outside their control and changes that people made themselves. What kind of changes did Ruth experience? What can a person do to change their own life?

> **Critical Thinking Tip:** Notice when a writer quotes someone. Ask yourself why the writer wants to use that person's words. What do they add to the story?

WRITING

A. Use the Target Vocabulary: Choose five target words or phrases from the list on page 80. On a piece of paper, use each word or phrase in a sentence. Underline the target vocabulary. Then find a partner and read each other's sentences.

B. Practice Writing: Choose one of these topics and write a short paragraph about it. Then find a partner and read each other's paragraphs.

1. Ruth's teachers encouraged her to go to college. Who encourages you? What do they encourage you to do? You can begin:

   _____ *encourage(s) me to* _____.
   (He/She/They) always tell(s) me...

2. Underline a part of Ruth Simmons's life story that you want to say something about. Why did you choose this part of her story? What does it mean to you? You can begin your paragraph:

   In "An Amazing Woman," the writer says, "..."

   or

   In "An Amazing Woman," Ruth Simmons is quoted as saying, "...".

> **Writing Tip:** Use *encourage* + someone + a verb in the infinitive (*to* + the base form of the verb): *My parents encouraged me to believe in myself.*

UNIT 2

Checkpoint

LEARNING OUTCOME

› Review and expand on the content of Unit 2

LOOK BACK

A. Think About This

Look back at your answers to the *Think About This* question on page 49: *Which of these life changes have you experienced?*

Do you want to add anything new?

B. Remember the Readings

What do you want to remember most from the readings in Unit 2? For each chapter, write one sentence about the reading.

Chapter 5: Life Is Full of Surprises

_____

Chapter 6: "It Was Love, So Strong and So Real"

_____

Chapter 7: To Live as an Artist

_____

Chapter 8: An Amazing Woman

_____

REVIEWING VOCABULARY

A. Three words in each group are nouns, verbs, or adjectives. Cross out the word that does not belong.

1. talent   wise   patience   stage
2. role   lesson   awful   career
3. energy   responsibility   suddenly   marriage
4. discover   stare   difference   manage
5. aware   secure   control   alike

B. Complete the sentences with words or phrases from the box. There are two extra words or phrases.

after all	a great deal	end up	give up	no longer
against the law	although	except	instead of	was about to

1. It is _____ not to pay your taxes.

2. _____ he was tired, he stayed at his desk and studied.

3. That painter has _____ of talent.

4. Everyone in the class is here _____ Kimiko. She'll be back tomorrow.

5. We should get her a present. _____, she's been very good to us.

6. It used to be important to me, but it _____ matters.

7. She was late to meet me. I had my phone in my hand and I _____ call her when she finally arrived.

8. _____ depending on his parents' support, he's going to get a job.

EXPANDING VOCABULARY

Read the sentences. Notice how the **boldfaced** words are used. What part of speech are they? Add them to the chart of word families. Use the singular form of any plural noun and the base form of each verb.

1. The movie **amazed** everyone.

   I stared out the window in **amazement**.

   We've seen an **amazing** change in her.

2. He **challenged** his brother to a race.

   My new job will be a big **challenge**.

   It's a **challenging** game, and I need more practice.

3. These are **comfortable** shoes.

   The mother **comforted** her child.

   The hotel tries to offer all the **comforts** of home.

4. He promised we would not be **disappointed**.

   They'll just have to deal with the **disappointment**.

   I'm afraid I'll **disappoint** them.

5. The doctor gave us some **encouraging** news.

   My friends **encouraged** me to get up and dance.

   All he needs is a little **encouragement**.

6. Please **lead** the way.

   She's an experienced **leader**.

   What's the **leading** cause of car accidents?

7. What a **shocking** story!

   The news came as a **shock**.

   She **shocked** her parents with her green hair.

8. He lost a **valuable** ring.

   I **value** your opinion very much.

   His research is of great **value** to heart patients everywhere.

WORD FAMILIES		
Nouns	Verbs	Adjectives
1 amazement	amaze	
2		
3		
4		
5		
6		
7		
8		

A PUZZLE

There are 10 target words from Unit 2 in this puzzle. The words go across (→) and down (↓). Find the words and circle them. Then use them to complete the sentences below.

```
X  Z  P  M  X  M (S  C  O  R  E)
F  N  O  T  I  C  E  V  X  K  S
O  X  W  B  Q  M  X  J  Z  H  C
R  N  E  P  X  N  Q  M  V  P  A
W  U  R  P  M  A  T  T  E  R  P
A  L  E  A  D  X  H  X  K  O  E
R  S  Z  T  V  M  W  G  T  J  N
D  C  O  V  E  R  X  K  B  E  K
V  A  X  N  X  B  M  W  V  C  X
P  H  A  R  D  L  Y  M  H  T  Q
```

ACROSS

1. It doesn't _____ which way you do it.

2. 100% is a perfect _____ _score_ _____.

3. You must be hungry—you ate _____ anything.

4. Rose got her hair cut, but her husband didn't _____.

5. Don't look! Close your eyes and _____ them with your hands.

6. You go first, please. You _____ and I'll follow.

DOWN

1. How did the man _____ from prison?

2. The president has a great deal of _____.

3. We can't go back. We can only go _____.

4. Max is working on a _____ for his science class.

BUILDING DICTIONARY SKILLS

Finding Words in the Dictionary

> ### Dictionary Entries
>
> An **entry** in the dictionary is a word or phrase and all the information about it (its definition, example sentences, and so on). Entry words in the dictionary are in alphabetical order.
>
> Sometimes it is easy to find the word or phrase you are looking for because it has its own entry. Sometimes, however, you will find the word or phrase in the entry for a related word (a member of its word family).

Look at the dictionary entries below and answer the questions.

> **sud•den** /'sʌdn/ *adj* **1** done or happening quickly or in a way you did not expect: *We've had a **sudden change** of plans.* | *Don't make any sudden moves around the animals.* **2 all of a sudden** suddenly: *All of a sudden, the lights went out.*—**suddenness** n. [U]
>
> **sud•den•ly** /'sʌdnli/ adv quickly and in a way you did not expect: *She suddenly realized what she'd done.* | *Smith died suddenly of a heart attack.*

1. Do *sudden* and *suddenly* each have their own entries in the dictionary?   YES   NO

2. What other member of the word family can you find in the entry for *sudden?*

   _____

> **brave¹** /breɪv/ *adj* dealing with danger, pain, or difficult situations with courage ANT **cowardly**: *brave soldiers* | *her brave fight against cancer—* **bravely** adv

3. Do *brave* and *bravely* each have their own entries in the dictionary?   YES   NO

> **deal²** *v* (past tense and past participle **dealt** /dɛlt/) [I,T] **1** *also* **deal out** to give out playing cards to players in a game: *It's my turn to deal.* **2** to buy and sell illegal drugs: *He was arrested for dealing heroin.* **3 deal a blow (to sb/sth)** to harm someone or something: *The ban dealt a severe blow to local tourism.*
>
> **deal in** sth *phr. v* to buy and sell a particular product: *a business dealing in medical equipment*
>
> **deal with** sb/sth *phr. v* **1** to do what is necessary, especially in order to solve a problem: *Who's dealing with the new account?* **2** to succeed in controlling your feelings and being patient in a difficult situation: *I can't deal with any more crying children today.* **3** to do business with someone: *We've been dealing with their company for ten years.* **4** to be about a particular subject: *a book dealing with 20th-century art*

> **Vocabulary Tip:**
> Adverbs ending in *-ly* are often found at the end of the dictionary entry for the adjective in that word family. Phrasal verbs are often found at the end of the entry for the verb.

4. Does the phrasal verb *deal with* have its own entry in the dictionary?   YES   NO

5. What other phrasal verb do you find in the entry for *deal?* _____

Vocabulary Self-Test 1

Circle the letter of the word or phrase that best completes each sentence.

1. Chris works for an airline and _____ fly for free, so he saves money.
   a. affords   **b.** believes in   **c.** joins   **d.** gets to

2. You can do what you want. It's your _____.
   a. choice   **b.** fear   **c.** root   **d.** shock

3. There have already been a lot of problems, and _____ there will be more.
   a. no doubt   **b.** rather   **c.** no longer   **d.** forward

4. The movie was so _____ that Matt fell asleep.
   a. popular   **b.** professional   **c.** boring   **d.** total

5. How long will it take for this letter to _____ Australia?
   a. accept   **b.** notice   **c.** stare   **d.** reach

6. In the game of "hide and seek," one child closes his eyes while the other children _____. Then he tries to find them.
   a. melt   **b.** hide   **c.** expect   **d.** matter

7. I'd like to go out and do something this evening, but I have nothing _____ in mind.
   a. specific   **b.** bored   **c.** alike   **d.** dusty

8. After failing two tests, David was in _____ of failing the course.
   a. value   **b.** support   **c.** patience   **d.** danger

9. Your baby is growing fast! How much does she _____?
   a. lead   **b.** weigh   **c.** prepare   **d.** find

10. Tina usually drives to work, but today she rode her bike _____.

    a. instead   **b.** against   **c.** except   **d.** wise

11. I have to _____ what's wrong with my computer before I can fix it.

    a. end up   **b.** figure out   **c.** turn out   **d.** get back to

12. The judge explained the _____ for her decision.

    a. medicine   **b.** score   **c.** basis   **d.** culture

13. *Exciting* is the _____ of *boring*.

    a. researcher   **b.** energy   **c.** opposite   **d.** variety

14. Jan _____ the name of the company, but I can't remember it.

    a. mentioned   **b.** faced   **c.** disappeared   **d.** rushed

15. The _____ U.S. family in the 1950s had four children.

    a. average   **b.** natural   **c.** brave   **d.** international

16. Many _____ of the city are not safe for people out walking at night.

    a. areas   **b.** responsibilities   **c.** roles   **d.** members

17. _____ I don't know much about it, I think I'd like to see that movie.

    a. Once   **b.** Although   **c.** In general   **d.** After all

18. He's never had this problem before, and he doesn't know how to _____ it.

    a. turn into   **b.** produce   **c.** encourage   **d.** deal with

19. The police officer kept his dog under _____ at all times.

    a. attack   **b.** stage   **c.** control   **d.** challenge

20. That young singer has so much _____ that she's sure to become a star.

    a. career   **b.** talent   **c.** tax   **d.** marriage

21. Only one part of the government has the _____ to make new laws.

    a. project   **b.** seed   **c.** enemy   **d.** power

22. Please speak up! We can _____ hear you.

    a. hardly   **b.** however   **c.** suddenly   **d.** a great deal

23. Let's go inside. I think it _____ rain.

    a. shares   **b.** is about to   **c.** manages   **d.** escapes

24. What's the _____ between the old plan and the new one?

    a. case   **b.** interview   **c.** difference   **d.** lesson

25. Before you start painting,_____ the floor with something to protect it.

    a. cover   **b.** stare   **c.** serve   **d.** consider

26. Pietro has visited _____ every country in South America.

    a. lonely   **b.** nearly   **c.** highly   **d.** naturally

27. I am not _____ of any problems with the machine.

    a. amazing   **b.** disappointed   **c.** aware   **d.** comfortable

28. Most tickets have already been sold, but a few are still _____.

    a. terrible   **b.** awful   **c.** local   **d.** available

29. Thousands of people were in the streets to _____ in the celebration.

    a. suggest   **b.** give up   **c.** take part   **d.** discover

See the Answer Key on page 239.

94 will be a blank page

THE OCEAN

THINK ABOUT THIS

What was the topic of the last news report you saw or heard about the ocean?

Check ☑ your answer.

- ☐ The ocean and the weather
- ☐ Something we get from the ocean
- ☐ Living things in the ocean
- ☐ Changes happening in the ocean
- ☐ Other: _____

CHAPTER 9

What Does the Ocean Mean to Us?

At the ocean

LEARNING OUTCOME

> Learn about the relationship between people and the ocean

GETTING READY TO READ

Talk about these questions in a small group.

1. How do you say "ocean" in your first language? What does this word make you think about? How does it make you feel? Why?

2. What makes people want to live near the ocean? What are some reasons people do *not* want to live near the ocean? What do you think about living near the ocean?

READING

Look at the words and definitions next to the reading. Then read without stopping.

What Does the Ocean Mean to Us?

1 Some people have no trouble explaining how the ocean is important in their lives. They live near it and depend on it for food. It gives them the work that supports their families. For people who live far from the ocean, the ways they are **connected** to it may not be so clear. However, if you know a few facts about the ocean, it's easy to see how important it is for *all* life on Earth. Did you know that the ocean covers 72 percent of the Earth's **surface**? It helps regulate the climate[1] by holding **heat** from the sun. It also **supplies** half of the **oxygen** in the air we breathe. The oxygen is produced by phytoplankton, tiny ocean plants that live just below the surface. These facts have led people to call the ocean Earth's "life support system."[2]

2 Did you know that eight of the world's ten largest cities are near the ocean? History explains why this is so. Cities began and grew on the **coast**, especially at the mouths of rivers,[3] because the ocean was so important for food and transport.[4] Today, almost half the people in the world live near the ocean.

3 **While** facts like these explain why the ocean matters, they do not answer another question: How does the ocean make us feel? The ocean has a strong effect on people's **emotions**. It can cause fear—of what we cannot see and do not know, of things that live in the ocean, or of big **storms**, like hurricanes and typhoons. It **makes sense** to be afraid of those. But the ocean can also make us feel **calm** and **relaxed**. How does it do that? Why do so many vacationers[5] want to be at the ocean? Why do people pay so much to live where they can see it? What is it that **draws** us to the ocean?

4 Many of us are drawn to it to have fun. We want to swim in it or go out in boats. Think of all the ways people have invented to play in and on the water! Others just want to be near the ocean. Perhaps it's because of the great open space, where we can see miles of open water and sky. Some say the space makes them feel free and full of hope. Others love the ever-changing colors of the sea. Still others are drawn by its sound. The crash of waves against rocks is exciting, while the **gentle** sound of small **waves** on the beach is calming and comforting.

5 Perhaps what draws people to the ocean is even more basic. Did you know that our brains are about 73 percent water? The answer to the question of what draws us to the sea may lie in the mysteries[6] of the human body.

[1] *regulate the climate* = control weather conditions around the world

[2] *life support system* = equipment for keeping someone alive (usually, in a hospital)

[3] *mouths of rivers* = the places where rivers meet the ocean

[4] *transport* = ways of taking people and things from one place to another

[5] *vacationers* = people taking a trip as a break from work or school

[6] *mysteries* = things that are unknown and cannot be explained

6   Many of us choose to be near the ocean when we can. We love seeing the ocean, hearing it, smelling it, playing in it, walking or sitting by it. We may not know why we feel the way we do about it. However, we do know how every person on Earth is connected to the ocean and how important that relationship is.

Quick Comprehension Check

A. Read these sentences **about the reading**. Circle T (true) or F (false). On the line, write the number of the paragraph with the answer.

1. There is more water than land on the Earth's surface.   T   F   _____

2. The human brain is almost half water.   T   F   _____

3. The ocean helps control how hot or cold the Earth gets.   T   F   _____

4. The ocean takes oxygen out of the air.   T   F   _____

5. Big storms make people love the ocean.   T   F   _____

6. People may not be able to explain their own feelings about the ocean.   T   F   _____

B. Work with your class. Share your answers from part A. Go back to the reading to find the reason why a sentence is true or false. Correct the false sentences.

EXPLORING VOCABULARY

Thinking about the Target Vocabulary

A. Look at the chart with the target vocabulary. Seven nouns are missing. Scan the reading to find them, and add them to the correct places in the chart. Write the singular form of any plural noun.

¶	Nouns	Verbs	Adjectives	Other
1		connect		
		supply		
2				
3				while

¶	Nouns	Verbs	Adjectives	Other
				make sense
			calm	
			relaxed	
		draw		
4			gentle	

B. Which words and phrases are new to you? Circle them in the list. Then find them in the reading. Look at the context. Can you guess the meaning?

Using the Target Vocabulary

A. These sentences are **about the reading**. Complete them with the words or phrases in the box.

calm	draws	heat	supplies	waves
connect	gentle	makes sense	surface	while

1. All human beings are in a relationship with the ocean. Many things

   _____ us to the ocean.

2. The ocean covers 72 percent of the _____, or outside

   layer, of the Earth.

   > **Vocabulary Tip:** *The surface of the ocean* means the top of the ocean where it meets the air.

3. The sun keeps the Earth warm. It gives us _____.

4. We get many things from the ocean. For example, it gives us oxygen.

   It _____ half the oxygen in the air we breathe.

5. The reading presents some facts about the ocean.

   _____ those facts explain how important the ocean is

   for life on Earth, they do *not* explain how the ocean makes us feel.

   > **Reading Tip:** *While* at the beginning of a sentence tells you the sentence will have two parts. Figure out if they have a relationship in time (*While I was out, it started to rain*) or show a contrast (see sentence 5).

6. Hurricanes and typhoons are dangerous, so it _____

   to be afraid of them. People *should* be afraid—and so be careful.

7. Sometimes being at the ocean makes us excited or afraid—when there are strong winds, for example. At other times, it has the opposite effect. When the sea is quiet and we have no worries, we feel _____.

8. Something that interests us may make us want to go closer. It _____ us to it. The ocean does this to many vacationers, for example.

9. Sometimes the ocean is loud, and we are very aware of its power. At other times, when it makes only quiet sounds, it seems _____.

10. Sometimes the ocean looks flat, but at other times, you can see lines of water that move across its surface. Those are _____.

B. These sentences use the target words and phrases **in new contexts**. Complete them with the words in the box.

calm	drawn	heat	supplied	waves
connects	gentle	made no sense	surface	while

1. Some animals that live in the ocean have to come up to the _____ to breathe.

2. When the weather gets cold, I turn on the _____ in my home.

3. The Panama Canal _____ the Atlantic Ocean to the Pacific Ocean in Central America.

4. Pablo fell asleep to the sound of the _____ hitting the beach.

5. People whose jobs carry a lot of responsibility need to deal with emergencies without getting excited. They need to stay _____ to make good decisions.

> **Vocabulary Tip:** *Calm* can also describe the ocean. When it's calm, there are no waves.

6. Maria's parents wanted her to join the family business, but Maria was _____ to a career in medicine instead.

7. The city _____ a piece of land and some seeds, but all the work on the garden was done by local people.

8. Be careful how you hold the baby! You must be _____ with babies.

9. No one understood what the scientist was talking about. It _____ to them.

Vocabulary Tip: *While* can be a synonym for *although*. (Synonyms are words with the same meaning.) Check your dictionary for other meanings of *while*.

10. _____ it's not easy to get work as an actor, our son has a great deal of talent, so we encouraged him to try.

C. Read the sentences. Guess the meaning of the **boldfaced** target words from the context. Match them with their definitions.

   a. There are some amazing beaches on the **coast** of Australia.
   b. I managed to sound **relaxed** during my job interview, but I felt nervous.
   c. The fishing boats returned home because a terrible **storm** was coming.
   d. Fear is a powerful **emotion**.
   e. The doctor gave the patient extra **oxygen** to breathe.

Target Word   **Definition**

1. _____ = a strong human feeling, such as love or hate

2. _____ = the area where the land meets the ocean

3. _____ = feeling comfortable and not worried

4. _____ = a gas in the air that all forms of animal and plant life need to live

5. _____ = a time of very bad weather with strong winds, rain, snow or dust, and sometimes lightning

Building on the Vocabulary

Word Grammar: *Ocean* and *Sea*

Using *Ocean*

- *The ocean* means the whole area of salt water that covers much of the Earth's surface.
- There are five large areas of salt water that are named oceans: the Pacific Ocean, the Atlantic Ocean, the Indian Ocean, the Southern Ocean, and the Arctic Ocean.

Using *Sea*

- *The sea* often means *the ocean: Why are people drawn to the sea/the ocean?*
- There are many named seas, all smaller than any named ocean: the Mediterranean Sea, the South China Sea, the Caribbean Sea, the Sea of Japan, etc.
- Use *sea*, not *ocean*, in these phrases:

    *They traveled both on land and **by sea** (= by ship on the ocean).*

    *The fishing boats spend weeks **at sea** (= on the ocean far from land).*

- *Sea* is often used before another noun, as in *seafood, sea level* (the average height of the ocean), and *sea creatures* (animals that live in the ocean).

Complete the sentences. Write *ocean* or *sea*.

1. The Pacific is the largest _____.

2. The Caribbean _____ is larger than the Mediterranean.

3. The waves at the beach were big because of a storm at _____.

4. The top of Mount Everest in the Himalayas is 29,035 feet above

    _____ level.

5. The _____ covers 72 percent of the Earth's surface.

DEVELOPING YOUR READING SKILLS

Topics of Paragraphs

Look at the list of paragraph topics from "What Does the Ocean Mean to Us?" Find the paragraph on each topic in the reading. Write the paragraph number (1–6).

a. the ocean and our emotions   Paragraph ____

b. reasons people want to be at the ocean   Paragraph ____

c. how important the ocean is   Paragraph ____

d. our bodies and the ocean   Paragraph ____

e. numbers of people living near the ocean   Paragraph ____

f. what we do and do not know about our relationship
    with the ocean   Paragraph ____

Main Ideas

A. Which paragraph best explains the main idea of the reading? Check ☑ your answer.

☐ Paragraph 1

☐ Paragraph 2

☐ Paragraph 6

B. Write one or two sentences that give the main idea of the reading in your own words.

_____

_____

C. What is the main idea of paragraph 3 in the reading? Check ☑ your answer.

☐ 1. There are many good reasons for people's fear of the ocean.

☐ 2. The ocean has power over our feelings because we depend on it.

☐ 3. While we are sometimes afraid of the ocean, it also has a strong pull on us.

Using Graphic Organizers

A Concept Map

A **concept map** (or *idea web)* is a type of graphic organizer. It can help you identify important ideas from a reading and show how they connect or relate.

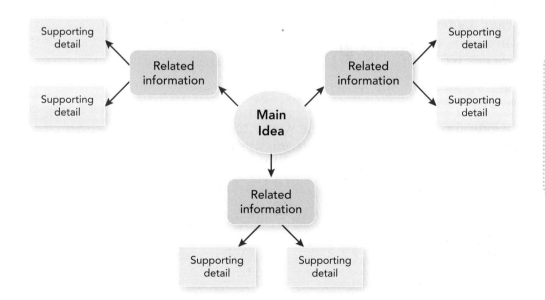

Critical Thinking Tip: When you choose information from a reading and enter it into a graphic organizer, you will often understand and remember the information better.

On a piece of paper, copy the concept map below. Complete the map by adding more circles and information from the reading about why the ocean is important and how people are drawn to it.

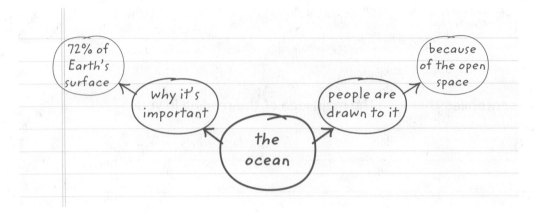

CRITICAL THINKING

Discussion

Talk about these questions with your class.

1. What two groups of people does the writer describe in paragraph 1? How are they different? Do you belong to one of these groups? Explain your answer.

2. The five senses are hearing, sight, smell, taste, and touch. The writer describes ways that the ocean has an effect on people through their senses. Can you find an example in the reading for each of the five? What other examples can you add?

3. In paragraph 4, the writer invites you to think about "all the ways people have invented to play in and on the water." How many can you name? Which ones have you experienced? Which ones might you like to do in the future?

4. Do you agree that people are drawn to the ocean? Do you feel drawn to the ocean yourself? Explain your answer.

5. What are the two questions about the ocean that the writer tries to answer in this reading? What information in the reading best answers each question? What information was new to you? What would you like to know more about?

WRITING

A. Use the Target Vocabulary: Choose five target words or phrases from the list on pages 98–99. On a piece of paper, use each word or phrase in a sentence. Then find a partner and read each other's sentences.

B. Practice Writing: Choose one of these topics and write a short paragraph about it. Then find a partner and read each other's paragraphs.

1. Do you agree or disagree that the "ocean has a strong effect on people's emotions" (paragraph 3)? Explain your answer, giving specific examples.

2. Choose a different sentence, or part of a sentence, from the reading to write about. You can begin, *In "What Does the Ocean Mean to Us," the writer says,* "... ." Copy the writer's words. Then explain your thoughts about this part of the reading.

> **Writing Tip:** When you take a sentence, or part of one, from a reading to use in your own writing, remember to copy carefully and put quotation marks before and after the other writer's words.

CHAPTER 10

The Crab

Christmas Island red crabs*

LEARNING OUTCOME

> Learn about an unusual animal that depends on the ocean

GETTING READY TO READ

Take a survey of your class.

How many people in the class have ever:

seen a crab on the beach? _____

seen a crab underwater? _____

eaten a crab? _____

cooked a crab? _____

had a crab as a pet? _____

been bitten by a crab? _____

watched a crab climb a tree? _____

* Every year, 120 million Christmas Island red crabs travel from the rainforest to the ocean.

READING

Look at the words, definitions, and pictures next to the reading. Then read without stopping.

The Crab

1 Introduction

Someone with an **interest** in sea creatures[1] could easily spend their **entire** life studying crabs. The crab is one of the oldest living types of animals, and there are about 4,500 kinds of them. Among all these crabs, there are many differences, but there are **certain** things that all crabs **have in common**.

[1] *sea creatures = animals that live in the ocean*

2 Ways That All Crabs Are Alike

- All crabs are invertebrates. That means they have no backbone. (Did you know that invertebrates **make up** about 95 percent of all known animals?)

- All crabs have a hard **shell**, called an exoskeleton.

- They have ten legs, with five on each side, and they have an unusual way of walking. Crabs can go forward or back but usually move sideways.[2]

- The first, or front, pair of a crab's legs are its claws. (See the photo.)

A Japanese Blue Crab shows its claws.

[2] *Crabs are known for moving sideways.*

3 Some Differences Among Crabs

- Not all crabs are sea creatures. Some types of crabs do live underwater, but others live on land, and some can live in either **environment**. Some manage to survive[3] in the hot water near underwater volcanoes,[4] while others live under the ice in Antarctica.

- Crabs are often the same color as their environment. The most common colors are gray, brown, and white. However, some crabs are beautiful reds, blues, and purples.

- Some crabs are herbivores (plant-eaters), others are carnivores (meat-eaters), and others are omnivores (plant- and meat-eaters).

[3] *survive = manage to live*

[4] *a volcano*

4 Did You Know?

- Christmas Island red crabs must put their eggs into the ocean so that the baby crabs can hatch (come out of the egg). The adult crabs cannot swim or breathe underwater. That makes it a dangerous business to be a mother!

- The largest crab in the world, the Japanese Spider Crab, can be **up to** four meters across (about 13 feet). The smallest is the pea crab. It's about the size of—can you guess?

- The largest land crab is the robber crab, or coconut crab. It can climb trees to pick coconuts.[5] Its claws are strong and **sharp** enough that it can open the coconuts, too.

- The crab in the photo on page 107, the Japanese Blue Crab, is the kind of crab most often eaten.

[5] *coconuts*

5 An Especially Helpful Crab

The tiny trapeziid crab (only one centimeter long, or ⅓ of an inch) helps keep coral reefs[6] **alive**. It cleans **dirt** from the reefs, letting the coral get the sunlight it needs to live. Today, much of the coral in the ocean is dying, so we should be glad for any help it can get.

[6] *coral reefs = See the photo of a coral reef on page 127.*

6 The Last Word on Crabs

If someone calls you crabby, they are not paying you a compliment.[7] A person who is crabby seems unhappy and often **complains**. They might always be like that, or they might get that way only at certain times. Some of us get crabby when we are tired or hungry or have too much work to do. It may not be **fair** to the poor crab to use its name this way, but English speakers have been doing it since the 1700s and will probably **go on** doing it. So the crab will just have to **put up with** it.

[7] *paying you a compliment = telling you something nice about yourself*

Quick Comprehension Check

A. Read these sentences **about the reading**. Circle T (true) or F (false). On the line, write the number of the paragraph with the answer.

1. Some crabs can climb trees.   T   F   _____
2. Crabs live in a wide variety of places.   T   F   _____
3. Most crabs have ten legs.   T   F   _____
4. Crabs always walk sideways.   T   F   _____
5. Crabs eat only plants.   T   F   _____
6. Crabby people are fun to be with.   T   F   _____

B. Work with your class. Share your answers from part A. Go back to the reading to find the reason why a sentence is true or false. Correct the false sentences.

EXPLORING VOCABULARY

Thinking about the Target Vocabulary

A. Look at the chart with the target vocabulary. Three phrasal verbs and four adjectives are missing. Scan the reading to find them, and add them to the correct places in the chart. Write the base form of each verb.

¶	Nouns	Verbs	Adjectives	Other
1	interest			
				certain
				have in common
2				
	shell			
3	environment			
4				up to
5				
	dirt			
6		complain		

B. Which words and phrases are new to you? Circle them in the list. Then find them in the reading. Look at the context. Can you guess the meaning?

Using the Target Vocabulary

A. These sentences are **about the reading**. What is the meaning of each **boldfaced** word or phrase? Circle a, b, or c.

Vocabulary Tip:
Interest can be a noun or a verb. See your dictionary for other meanings of the noun.

1. Someone with an **interest** in crabs can study more than 4,000 kinds of them. An interest in something is a feeling of wanting to

   a. eat it.   **b.** turn into it.   **c.** know more about it.

2. Some scientists spend their **entire** careers researching crabs. *Entire* means

   a. lonely, sad.   **b.** whole, complete.   **c.** calm, patient.

3. Every crab **has** some things **in common with** other crabs. *Have something in common with someone* means

   a. have a problem with them.
   b. have the same thing they do.
   c. be the opposite of them.

4. Different types of crabs live in different **environments**. An animal's environment is

   a. the kind of place it lives in.
   b. a place to hide.
   c. its family group.

5. One type of crab can be **up to** four meters across (about 13 feet). *Up to* means

   a. equal to or less than.
   b. a great deal of.
   c. more than.

6. Don't shake hands with a robber crab. Their claws are very strong and **sharp**. *Sharp* means

   a. with a thin edge that can cut.
   b. wise.
   c. showing a lot of talent.

7. When the trapeziid crab helps clean off a reef, it helps keep the coral **alive** because coral will die if it can't get sunlight. *Alive* means

   a. clean.   **b.** local.   **c.** living.

8. Crabby people seem unhappy and often **complain**. If you complain about something, you

   a. are annoyed or upset about it.
   b. believe in it.
   c. are in shock over it.

9. Crabs aren't crabby, so it doesn't seem **fair** to use their name that way. *Fair* means

   a. calm, relaxed.   **b.** acceptable, right.   **c.** awful, terrible.

10. People probably won't stop using the word *crabby*, so crabs will have to **put up with** it. When you put up with something, you

    a. figure it out.
    b. take part in it.
    c. accept it without complaining.

B. These sentences use the target words and phrases **in new contexts**. Complete them with the words in the box.

alive	entire	fair	interest	sharp
complain	environment	have something in common	put up with	up to

1. It's amazing that no one was hurt in the accident. Everyone is

   _____ and well.

2. They _____: They both love good food and hate to

   rush through a meal.

3. Monique doesn't like snow, but she lives in Montreal, so she has to

   _____ it.

4. Be careful with that knife. It's very _____.

5. The job was rather boring, but Max didn't _____. He just did

   his work and accepted it.

6. Did you really manage to eat that _____ pizza?

7. You've done all the work on the project, with no help from your team. It

   hardly seems _____.

8. We can afford to give _____ $50 to support the group's work,

   but not more than that.

9. I've been reading a lot about the case. I took an _____ in it

   after hearing about it on the news.

10. The phrase "the _____" means the air, land, and water in

    which all the people, animals, and plants on Earth live.

> **Vocabulary Tip:**
> The adjective *alive* cannot come before a noun. Use it after *be* or another linking verb. Other adjectives like this are *afraid*, *alike*, *alone*, *asleep*, *awake*, and *aware*.

C. Read the sentences. Guess the meaning of the **boldfaced** target words and phrases from the context. Match them with their definitions.

a. We wash our clothes to get the **dirt** out.

b. Some people go to the beach to collect **shells**.

c. The 206 bones in the human body **make up** a person's skeleton.

d. Some fruits are available only at **certain** times of the year.

e. I won't give up! I'll **go on** trying until I succeed.

Target Word or Phrase	Definition
1. _____ =	something that makes things not clean, like dust
2. _____ =	continue
3. _____ =	come together and form a group or system
4. _____ =	the hard outer part that covers and protects some animals
5. _____ =	used to talk about a specific person, thing, group, etc. without naming or describing them

> **Vocabulary Tip:**
> The phrasal verb *make up* has many meanings. Read about them in your dictionary. Look for *make up* at the end of the entry for *make*.

Building on the Vocabulary

Word Grammar: *Certain*

- Use *certain* + noun to mean a specific person, thing, group, etc., that is not named.

  Certain people at work are hard for me to deal with.

- Use *certain* after *be* or another linking verb to mean "sure, confident, without having any doubts."

  Olivia was certain she had done well in the interview.

  When *certain* means "sure," it cannot come before a noun.

  This sentence is correct: *The man was certain that he was right.*

  This sentence is incorrect: *He was a ~~certain~~ man.*

Read the sentences. Does *certain* mean "specific" or "sure"? Circle your answers.

1.	Ali seemed certain of the facts.	specific	sure
2.	Do people in cross-cultural marriages face certain challenges?	specific	sure
3.	No one is certain how the man escaped.	specific	sure
4.	Leaders need certain talents.	specific	sure

DEVELOPING YOUR READING SKILLS

Understanding Text Features

Text Features: Subheadings

Each part of the reading "The Crab" has its own title, or **subheading**. Subheadings help you see how the information in a text is organized. They tell you what to expect in each section of the text.

Match the six subheadings from "The Crab" with the main ideas of the six sections of the text. Write the letters.

Reading Tip:
When a text has subheadings, read those first. They tell you something about the main ideas so you understand the text better as you read.

_____ 1. Introduction

_____ 2. Ways That All Crabs Are Alike

_____ 3. Some Differences Among Crabs

_____ 4. Did You Know?

_____ 5. An Especially Helpful Crab

_____ 6. The Last Word on Crabs

a. The trapeziid crab helps coral reefs by cleaning dirt from them.

b. The 4,500 kinds of crab are alike in some ways and different in others.

c. There are certain ways that crabs are different, as in their environments and eating habits.

d. There are certain things that all crabs have in common, such as a hard shell and claws.

e. The crab has given its name to an English word (_crabby_) that people have been using since the 1700s.

f. There are many unusual crabs, such as one that can be 13 feet across and another the size of a pea.

Reading for Details

Are these statements about the reading true or false? If the reading doesn't give the information, check (✔) **_It doesn't say._**

	True	False	It doesn't say.
1. The crab is one of the oldest living types of animals.			
2. An invertebrate is an animal that has no backbone.			
3. Crabs can move fastest if they go sideways.			
4. Herbivore crabs eat other crabs.			
5. The Japanese Spider Crab lives underwater.			
6. The Japanese Blue Crab is smaller than the pea crab.			
7. A person who is crabby looks like a crab.			

Definitions

Writing Definitions

Sometimes a reading gives you a definition of a new word or phrase. Especially in textbooks, you will find definitions of words that are important both for understanding a reading and for further study of that subject.

A common sentence pattern for definitions of nouns is:

A/An _____ is a _____ who/that _____.
        (noun)

An invertebrate is an animal that has no backbone.

A professor is a person who teaches at a university and does research.

Complete the definitions using information from the reading. Use the sentence pattern from the box above.

> **Reading Tip:** Look for definitions in the reading itself and in margin notes.

1. __An__ herbivore *is an animal that* _____

2. _____ carnivore _____

3. _____ omnivore _____

Main Ideas and Supporting Details

A. Read the three statements that give main ideas from the reading. Then read the details. Which details support each main idea? Write them on the lines.

1. All crabs have certain things in common.

   They are invertebrates. _____

   _____

2. Crabs can survive in a variety of environments.

   _____

   _____

3. There are other differences among types of crabs, too.

   _____

   _____

   DETAILS

   a. Their shells can be a variety of colors.

   b. Crabs manage to live in very cold and hot water.

   c. They are invertebrates.

    d. They have a hard shell and claws.

    e. Some eat plants, some eat meat, and some eat both.

    f. Some live on land, some underwater, and some can do either.

B. Write two details from the reading that support the statement below.
Some facts about crabs are rather surprising.

_____

_____

CRITICAL THINKING

Discussion

Talk about these questions in a small group.

1. Most of the language in "The Crab" is general English, but there are a few technical terms. *Technical terms* means very specific words of the kind used by people who know a lot about a subject. In this case, they are scientific terms relating to animals. For example, the writer says "Some crabs are herbivores (plant-eaters), others are carnivores (meat-eaters), and others are omnivores (plant- and meat-eaters)." What is the purpose of the parentheses in this sentence?

   Look at the section "Did You Know?" and the section "An Especially Helpful Crab." What is the purpose of the parentheses used in those sections? Can you find any other ways the writer uses parentheses in this reading?

   > **Critical Thinking Tip:** Notice how writers use parentheses to add information that may help you understand something they have said.

2. What do you think *business* means in the phrase "a dangerous business"? What do Christmas Island red crabs do that is dangerous for them? Use information from the reading and also from the photo and footnote on page 106 to support your answer.

3. What does the reading say is special about the trapeziid crab? What does the reading say is happening to coral? What do you think might be causing the problem?

4. Why does the writer use the phrase "the poor crab" in the section "The Last Word on Crabs"? Do you think the writer is being serious in this paragraph? Explain your answer.

5. On page 106, the writer says that in this chapter, you will learn about "an unusual animal." What facts in the reading best support the writer's idea that the crab is an unusual animal? What information in the reading surprised you? Did reading "The Crab" change any ideas you had about crabs? Explain your answer.

WRITING

A. Use the Target Vocabulary: Choose five target words or phrases from the list on page 109. On a piece of paper, use each word or phrase in a sentence. Then find a partner and read each other's sentences.

B. Practice Writing: Choose a topic and write a paragraph. Then find a partner and read each other's paragraphs.

1. Do some research about crabs. Find a fact about crabs that surprises you and that you think will surprise your classmates. Write a paragraph to explain what you found out. Include the source of your information (the title and author of the book or article or the address of the website).

2. Think of another animal that lives in or depends on the ocean. Do some research on it. Write a paragraph to report one or more interesting facts about it. Start by explaining why you chose this animal. You can begin:

   The (animal) interests me because . . . . One of the most interesting facts about the (animal) is that . . . .

   After your paragraph, list your sources (the titles and authors of books or articles or the website addresses).

> **Writing Tip:** When you write the title of a book, underline it (if you are writing by hand) or put it in *italics* (if you are typing on a computer).

CHAPTER 11

Cleaning Up the Ocean

Boyan Slat's invention

LEARNING OUTCOME

❯ Learn about efforts to deal with plastic in the sea

GETTING READY TO READ

Talk about these questions in a small group

1. Look at the photo. What do you think this invention does?

2. Have you heard of "garbage patches" in the ocean? What do you know about them? What questions would you ask about them?

3. The International Coastal Clean-up takes place one day every year in more than 100 countries. What do you know about it? What questions would you ask about it?

Read to Find Out: How are people trying to clean up the ocean?

Look at the words and definitions next to the reading. Then read without stopping.

Cleaning Up the Ocean

1   The Pacific Ocean **contains** more than half the water on the **planet**. It also holds a lot of trash, much of it plastic. There are plastic bottles, plastic bags, food wrappers,[1] and many other kinds of packaging.[2] Many of them were used only once before becoming trash and ending up in the ocean. Trillions[3] of pieces of plastic are **floating** in the Pacific, and more go into its waters each year.

2   All this trash is an ugly **mess**. It's an expensive problem, too. It costs billions of dollars each year to the fishing, shipping, and tourism industries.[4] More than that, it's dangerous. Every year, at least one million seabirds and many thousands of other animals die because of plastic **pollution**. People's health is also **affected** because the plastic is full of toxic chemicals.[5] Fish eat the plastic, and people eat the fish.

3   Some of the trash ends up on beaches. The United States spends about $500 million a year to clean up its West Coast beaches alone. Around the world, people are working to clean up the beaches in their own countries. Since 1986, hundreds of thousands of **volunteers** have joined the International Coastal Cleanup. On the day of the 2014 Cleanup, volunteers picked up more than 16 million pounds of trash.

4   Other people are trying to figure out how to get the plastic out of the ocean. This is what Boyan Slat is working on. At age 16, he started studying the problem. He soon invented a **system** for catching plastic floating on or near the surface.

5   At 19, Boyan left his university in the Netherlands to start a foundation,[6] The Ocean Cleanup. He now leads a large team of scientists and engineers. They are **developing** the **technology** to clean millions of pounds of plastic from the sea. Their goal is to clean up the largest "garbage patch" in the Pacific. They expect the job will take years. For his **efforts**, Boyan received the United Nations' highest environmental award.[7] The UN named him a Champion of the Earth.

Boyan Slat

[1] *food wrappers = pieces of plastic or paper that cover food when it is sold*

[2] *packaging = bags, boxes, etc., that contain products to be sold*

[3] *trillions = 2,000,000,000,000 or more*

[4] *industries = specific types of businesses, trades, or services*

[5] *toxic chemicals = substances that can kill*

[6] *a foundation = an organization that gives or collects money for a specific purpose, such as research*

[7] *environmental award = a prize for protecting the environment*

6 Boyan and his team are in a hurry to get plastic out of the ocean. Right now, most of it is in large pieces. However, sunlight is turning it into microplastics (very tiny pieces). Those are even more dangerous. They're also harder to collect.

7 Boyan does not believe that the system he invented will end the problem of "garbage patches" in the sea. He asks, "How are we now going to **make sure** no more plastic enters the oceans **in the first place**?" About eight million tons[8] of plastic go into the sea every year. More and more plastic bags, bottles, and food wrappers. More and more plastic cups, forks, knives, and spoons. What can we do?

[8] *tons* = a ton is equal to 2,000 pounds (907.2 kilograms)

8 People fighting the problem say one answer is to change laws. They want to make the producers of plastic take more responsibility for it. They say another way is for people to make small changes in how they live. Some people are trying to **make a difference** by:

- taking their own bags to the store instead of accepting plastic bags,
- buying products that can be re-used,
- **recycling** plastic and buying recycled products, and
- volunteering to clean up their own part of the planet.

Quick Comprehension Check

A. Read these sentences **about the reading.** Circle T (true) or F (false). On the line, write the number of the paragraph with the answer.

1. Plastic in the ocean is a problem for several reasons.   T   F   _____

2. The biggest pieces of plastic are the biggest problem.   T   F   _____

3. International Coastal Cleanup volunteers take plastic out of the sea.   T   F   _____

4. Boyan Slat studied ocean pollution at a U.S. university.   T   F   _____

5. Boyan invented a system to clean plastic off the ocean floor.   T   F   _____

6. A lot of plastic products are probably going into the sea today.   T   F   _____

B. Work with your class. Share your answers from part A. Go back to the reading to find the reason why a sentence is true or false. Correct the false sentences.

EXPLORING VOCABULARY

Thinking about the Target Vocabulary

A. Look at the chart with the target vocabulary. Seven nouns are missing. Scan the reading to find them, and add them to the correct places in the chart. Write the singular form of any plural noun.

¶	Nouns	Verbs	Adjectives	Other
1		contain		
		float		
2				
		affect		
3				
4				
5		develop		
7				make sure
				in the first place
8				make a difference
		recycle		

B. Which words and phrases are new to you? Circle them in the list. Then find them in the reading. Look at the context. Can you guess the meaning?

Using the Target Vocabulary

A. These sentences are **about the reading.** Complete them with the target words and phrases in the box.

affects	develop	floats	make sure	system
contains	efforts	in the first place	mess	the planet

1. The Pacific Ocean holds a lot of water. It _____ more than half the water on Earth.

2. The Pacific Ocean is one of five oceans on _____.

3. No doubt some of the trash in the Pacific is deep down on the ocean floor, but much of the plastic _____ on or near the surface of the water.

Vocabulary Tip: *A planet* means one of the large round objects that move around the sun like Earth, Mars, etc. *The planet* means Earth when talking about the environment.

4. The plastic floating in the Pacific forms "garbage patches." They're a terrible sight. The writer calls all this trash "an ugly _____."

5. Plastic is not food. In fact, it's dangerous to eat. But fish eat the plastic, and people eat the fish, so the ocean pollution _____ people's health.

6. Boyan Slat thought of a way to take plastic out of the ocean. He has a _____ for doing this.

7. It is the job of the scientists and engineers at The Ocean Cleanup to _____ the system Boyan invented and try to improve it over time.

Vocabulary Tip: *Affect* is usually a verb: *How did the problem affect you? Effect* is usually a noun: *What effect did it have on you?*

8. Boyan has worked hard to try to do something about the problem of ocean pollution. He won a UN award for these _____ .

9. Boyan asks what actions we can take to be certain that plastic stops going into the ocean. He wants to _____ that it stops.

10. It will be great if Boyan's invention works to clean plastic out of the ocean, but plastic should not be going into the ocean _____.

B. These sentences use the target words and phrases **in new contexts.** Complete them with the words and phrases in the box.

affects	developing	float	make sure	system
contains	effort	in the first place	mess	the planet

1. *Climate change* means changes on _____ that are making the ocean and the rest of the environment warmer.

2. Ocean pollution _____ everyone in the world. No one is free from its effects.

3. Chocolate _____ more than 300 chemicals, and some affect the human brain.

4. Something that contains a lot of air will probably _____ when you put it in the water.

5. The company spends a great deal of money _____ new products that will draw new customers.

6. The purpose of a life support _____ is to keep someone alive when they are very sick.

7. The interview will start at 10 o'clock. Please _____ you're on time.

8. He was very sure about his decision, so we made no _____ to change his mind.

9. After the storm, the entire island was a _____. The cleanup took months.

10. I'm glad he wasn't hurt in the accident, but he shouldn't have been driving my car _____!

> **Writing Tip:**
> Use *in the first place* at the end of a sentence to stress what was true or should have been done earlier.

C. Read each definition and look at the paragraph number. Look back at the reading on pages 118–119 to find the **boldfaced** word or phrase to match the definition. Copy it in the chart.

Definition	Paragraph	Target Word or Phrase
1. things that make air, water, soil, etc., dangerously dirty	2	
2. people who help or work not for pay but because they want to	3	
3. new machines, equipment, and ways of doing things that are based on modern understanding of science	5	
4. have an effect, especially to improve something	8	
5. putting used objects or materials through a special process so that they can be used again	8	

> **Vocabulary Tip:** *Make a difference* is often used in the context of environmental or social problems, when people are trying to fix the problem. See your dictionary for other meanings.

Building on the Vocabulary

Collocations: *Do* and *Make* + Noun

Collocations are words that we often use together. Some words can go together and some cannot. *Do* and *make* are often used in collocations with certain words. For example, we can say, *Please make an effort to be on time,* but we can't say *Please do an effort . . . .*

Other verb + noun pairs are

> make + *a mess, a difference, a choice, a mistake, money*
>
> do + *a job, business, homework, the dishes*

Use *make* or *do* to complete each sentence.

1. When we do art projects with the children, we usually _____ a mess.

2. You can depend on Ruth to _____ a good job.

3. We _____ business with several companies in that area.

4. They hope to _____ a lot of money with the new technology.

5. Volunteers for the International Coastal Cleanup want to _____ a difference.

DEVELOPING YOUR READING SKILLS

Using Graphic Organizers

A Venn Diagram

Use a **Venn diagram** when you want to compare two people, things, ideas, or events. It makes it easy to see what the two have in common and what the differences are. In the part of the diagram on the left, write what is true for only one of the two. On the right, write what is true only for the other. In the middle, write what is true for both of them.

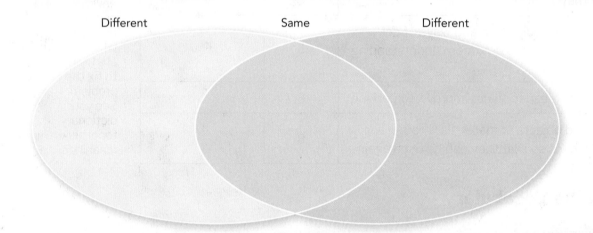

Different   Same   Different

On a piece of paper, draw a Venn diagram. Write notes in the spaces on the left and right to show differences between the International Coastal Cleanup and the Ocean Cleanup. Write notes in the space in the middle about the ways they are alike, such as, "Both want to save the environment."

Topics of Paragraphs

What is each paragraph in the reading about? Write the topics of the paragraphs.

1. Paragraph 1: _____

2. Paragraph 2: _____

3. Paragraph 3: _____

4. Paragraph 4: _____

5. Paragraph 5: _____

6. Paragraph 6: _____

7. Paragraph 7: _____

8. Paragraph 8: _____

> **Reading Tip:** When you read about several problems, as in paragraph 2, notice the order. Writers often start with the least serious problem and put the one they think most important last.

Summarizing

Write a summary of "Cleaning Up the Ocean." Write it as a paragraph. Include the answers to these questions:

What problem does the reading describe?

Why does it matter?

What are some people trying to do about it?

What do we still need to figure out?

You can begin: *The Pacific Ocean contains trillions of pieces of plastic.*

Writing Tip: Before you write a summary of a text, prepare to write by listing the topic of each paragraph, or section of the text, and the main idea about it.

CRITICAL THINKING

Discussion

Talk about these questions in a small group.

1. The reading says, "Every year, at least one million seabirds and many thousands of other animals die because of plastic pollution" (paragraph 2). Why do you think they die? What is the writer's opinion about this? How do you know? Do you agree? Explain your answer.

   Later, the reading says that microplastics "are even more dangerous" (paragraph 6). Dangerous for whom? Why do you think this is?

2. In paragraph 3, the writer reports that the United States is spending "about $500 million a year to clean up its West Coast beaches alone." What does *alone* mean in this context? Why do you think beach clean-ups cost so much? Do you think this is money well spent? Explain your answer.

3. Read paragraph 5 again. What do you think *Champion of the Earth* means? What do you think is the writer's purpose in giving this information about Boyan's award from the United Nations?

Critical Thinking Tip: Thinking about the writer's purpose can help you identify the writer's **point of view** (their personal opinion or way of thinking about something).

4. Read these definitions:

   - An optimist is a person who is always hopeful and believes good things will happen.

   - A pessimist is the opposite: Pessimists expect bad things to happen.

   Would you describe Boyan Slat as an optimist or a pessimist? Underline information in the reading that supports your opinion.

5. Read aloud the information in each part of the chart. What do you think about it? How does it make you feel?

September 20, 2014 International Coastal Cleanup	Plastic going into the ocean	Do the math
16,000,000 pounds of trash picked up from beaches by 56,000 volunteers in 91 countries	**over 16,000,000,000** pounds of plastic every year	To clean up all that plastic, you would need more than 1,000 one-day Coastal Cleanups each year.

Do you think the one-day-a-year International Coastal Cleanups make a difference? Explain your answer.

6. What five changes are mentioned in paragraph 8? Put the changes in order from *easiest to do* to *most difficult*. What other ideas could you add to the list?

> **Reading Tip:** The list on page *119* is a **bulleted list**. Bulleted lists are used to present information in an easy-to-read way. Notice how the four points in the list are alike in the way they are written.

WRITING

A. Use the Target Vocabulary: Choose five target words or phrases from the list on page 120. On a piece of paper, use each word or phrase in a sentence. Then find a partner and read each other's sentences.

B. Practice Writing: Choose a topic. Write a paragraph. Then find a partner and read each other's paragraphs.

1. Think of a person you know who is trying to make a difference. Describe what this person is trying to do. Then explain what you think about their efforts.

2. Some of the ideas in paragraph 8 of the reading are about asking people to change their habits. (A habit is something you do often, usually without thinking about it because you have done it so many times before.) Write about an experience you have had trying to change a habit.

> **Writing Tip:** When you use the phrase *make a difference* to mean "make things better," use the phrase alone or add *in* (+ something/a place) or *for* (+ someone/a group).

CHAPTER 12

Underwater Wonderland

Visitors to a coral reef

LEARNING OUTCOME

> Learn about coral reefs

GETTING READY TO READ

Read the statements about the Great Barrier Reef, one of the Seven Wonders of the Natural World.[1] Circle True or False. Talk about your answers with your class.

1.	The Great Barrier Reef is near the coast of Australia.	True	False
2.	It is about 600 miles (1000 kilometers) long.	True	False
3.	Astronauts can see it from space.	True	False
4.	The entire Great Barrier Reef is made of coral reefs.	True	False
5.	It has grown bigger every year for thousands of years.	True	False

[1] the Seven Wonders of the Natural World = seven of the most beautiful places on the planet

READING

Read to Find Out: What is happening to the Great Barrier Reef?

Look at the words, definitions, and pictures next to the reading. Then read without stopping.

Underwater Wonderland

1 The Great Barrier Reef, **off** the coast of Australia, draws people from all over the world. It's a beautiful place to swim, go boating, and relax on the beach. However, what is most special about the Great Barrier Reef is what you can see underwater.

2 The Great Barrier Reef is 1,400 miles long (over 2,200 kilometers). It's made up of almost 1,000 islands and nearly 3,000 coral reefs, making it the world's largest coral reef system. It's the only living thing on the planet that can be seen from **space**. The reefs were built over thousands of years by billions of tiny sea creatures[1] called coral polyps.

[1] *sea creatures* = animals that live in the ocean

3 It may be difficult to think of coral polyps as animals. They do not swim or move themselves across the ocean floor. They do not have eyes, ears, a heart, or a brain. A coral polyp is **basically** a tiny soft body with a mouth and a stomach. It also has tentacles that help it protect itself and catch food.

4 Some coral polyps live alone, but most live in groups called colonies. Each differently shaped part of a reef is its own colony. A colony has a single species, or type, of coral. In the Great Barrier Reef, there are about 400 species of coral **in all**.

A coral polyp can be from 0.25 to 12 inches tall (0.63 to 30.5 centimeters).

5 Most of the 400 are hard coral species, the type that builds reefs. They produce calcium carbonate—the same thing shells are made of—at the **base** of their bodies. They use it to **attach** themselves to a rock or the sea floor. Then it becomes hard, like a shell. Reefs are built over time, as coral produce more and more calcium carbonate. Reefs then **attract** many other types of sea creatures and plants. **Exactly** how many no one can say. Counting just the fish, the Great Barrier Reef is home to more than 1,500 species.

6 In 1975, the Australian government established[2] the Great Barrier Reef Marine Park. The **point** was to protect the reefs. However, these reefs, like coral reefs everywhere, are in danger. A great deal of the coral has already died. Researchers studying the **situation** found that between 1985 and 2012, the Great Barrier Reef had lost *half* its coral cover.[3]

[2] *establish* = start something (a company, university, system, etc.) that is expected to last a long time

[3] *coral cover* = living coral on the sea floor

7 **Violent** storms called cyclones **destroyed** many of the reefs. The researchers say storms caused about half the damage[4] to the coral. Climate change[5] could cause storms like these to hit more often. If they do, the coral cover won't have enough time between storms to grow back. The second largest problem was a growing number of crown-of-thorns starfish.[6] They eat coral polyps. Between 1985 and 2012, they ate them faster than the coral cover could grow back.

8 Coral everywhere face the problem of higher ocean temperatures caused by climate change. Some coral species cannot deal with the warmer waters. Then there is ocean pollution. No species deals well with that.

9 In the past few years, many countries have established new Marine Protected Areas (MPAs). That's great news. These are parts of the ocean that are like **national** parks on land. In an MPA, human **activities**—especially commercial fishing[7]—are controlled to protect the plants and animals. More MPAs are needed. Right now, only one percent of the ocean is protected in this way. However, even in MPAs, as in the Great Barrier Reef, **nature** is not safe from pollution or climate change.

[4] *damage* = a bad effect on something

[5] *climate change* = changes on the planet (largely caused by human activity) that are making the environment warmer

[6] a *starfish* (or sea star)

[7] *commercial fishing* = the business of catching and selling fish and other sea creatures

Quick Comprehension Check

A. Read these sentences **about the reading**. Circle T (true) or F (false). On the line, write the number of the paragraph with the answer.

1. The Great Barrier Reef is in international waters.   T   F   _____

2. The Great Barrier Reef is the largest coral reef system in the world.   T   F   _____

3. The reefs are made of calcium carbonate, like shells.   T   F   _____

4. The calcium carbonate comes from the bodies of coral polyps.   T   F   _____

5. Warmer ocean water is good for coral.   T   F   _____

6. Coral reefs all around the world are in danger.   T   F   _____

B. Work with your class. Share your answers from part A. Go back to the reading to find the reason why a sentence is true or false. Correct the false sentences.

EXPLORING VOCABULARY

Thinking about the Target Vocabulary

A. Look at the chart with the target vocabulary. Six nouns, three verbs, and two adjectives are missing. Scan the reading to find them, and add them to the correct places in the chart. Write the singular form of any plural noun. Write the base form of each verb.

¶	Nouns	Verbs	Adjectives	Other
1				off
2				
3				basically
4				in all
5				
				exactly
6				
7				
9				

B. Which words and phrases are new to you? Circle them in the list. Then find them in the reading. Look at the context. Can you guess the meaning?

Using the Target Vocabulary

A. These sentences are **about the reading**. What is the meaning of each **boldfaced** word or phrase? Circle a, b, or c.

1. The Great Barrier Reef is **off** the coast of Australia. Here, *off* means
   - **a.** a short distance from.
   - **b.** connected to.
   - **c.** up to.

2. A coral polyp is **basically** a body with a mouth, stomach, and tentacles. *Basically* means

   a. in the first place.   b. hardly.   c. in the main or most important ways.

3. The Great Barrier Reef has about 400 species of coral **in all.** *In all* means

   a. so far.   b. after all.   c. as a total.

4. A coral polyp puts out soft calcium carbonate at the **base** of its body. The base of something is

   a. the lowest or bottom part.   b. the surface.   c. the cover.

5. Coral polyps use calcium carbonate to **attach** themselves to a rock or the sea floor. *Attach* means

   a. float.   b. connect.   c. escape.

6. Coral reefs **attract** many types of sea creatures who are looking for food or places to hide. *Attract* means

   a. manage.   b. draw.   c. produce.

7. **The point of** establishing a marine park is to protect a part of the sea. The point of doing something is its

   a. effect.   b. result.   c. purpose.

8. Cyclones, typhoons, and hurricanes are all **violent** storms. *Violent* means happening with a lot of

   a. advanced technology.   b. dangerous power.   c. mess and pollution.

9. A Marine Protected Area is like a **national** park, but one is in the sea, the other on land. *National* means

   a. not yet developed.   b. popular.   c. belonging to a country.

> **Reading Tip:**
> Make sure to read the captions for photos and illustrations that go with a text. They may help you understand new vocabulary, like *tentacles.*

> **Vocabulary Tip:**
> *Point* has many meanings and uses. See your dictionary to learn more.

B. These sentences use the target words and phrases **in new contexts.** Complete them with the words and phrases in the box.

attach	base	in all	off	violent
attract	basically	national	point	

1. One role of the government is to protect our _____ interests.

2. I sometimes _____ a photo to an email message.

3. The two fish belong to different species, but _____, they look alike.

4. The hotel was on a quiet side street just _____ the main street.

5. The beautiful beaches _____ many visitors to the island.

Vocabulary Tip: *Attract* can mean to make someone go to, or move closer to, something. It can also mean to make someone feel interested in a person or thing.

6. There were _____ winds of over 100 miles per hour.

7. I sat down at the _____ of a tree and rested my back against it.

8. What did the researchers want to know? What was the _____ of their study?

9. Volunteers from 91 countries took part in the Coast Cleanup, nearly 60,000 of them _____.

C. Read the sentences. Guess the meaning of the **boldfaced** target words from the context. Match them with their definitions.

a. A "natural wonder" is something amazing found in **nature**.
b. Would you want to leave Earth and travel into **space**?
c. The enemy attacked the town and **destroyed** many buildings.
d. A quotation repeats **exactly** what someone said or wrote.
e. What is your favorite weekend **activity**?
f. He was unhappy with the **situation** at work and said he would no longer put up with it.

Vocabulary Tip: See your dictionary for other meanings of *nature*. Look up *natural* and *naturally* to learn how they relate to each meaning of nature.

Target Word	Definition
1. _____	= the area beyond Earth where the stars and other planets are
2. _____	= something that people do, because they enjoy it or to reach a goal
3. _____	= everything in the physical world not controlled by human beings, such as wild plants and animals and the weather
4. _____	= hurt something so badly that it is gone or cannot be used or fixed
5. _____	= used to stress that a number or piece of information is completely correct in every detail
6. _____	= all the things that are happening at a specific time in a specific place

Building on the Vocabulary

Word Grammar: Transitive and Intransitive Verbs

Some verbs are **transitive** ([T]). After a transitive verb, there must be a direct object (D.O.). It is usually a noun or pronoun.

         [T]   D.O.
Coral reefs attract fish. (NOT: "~~Coral reefs attract.~~" *Attract* needs a direct object.)

Some verbs are **intransitive** ([I]). After an intransitive verb, there can be no direct object.

           [I]
Plastic is light, so it floats. (NOT: "*Plastic is light, so ~~the ocean floats plastic.~~*" *Float* cannot take a direct object.)

Some verbs, like *develop*, can be either transitive or intransitive. Check your dictionary to learn if a verb can be both. Also, notice what abbreviations your dictionary uses for *transitive* and *intransitive*.

    He has developed a new system.   [T]

    A problem has developed.   [I]

Read the example sentences. Is the **boldfaced** verb transitive or intransitive in this sentence? Circle your answer.

> **Writing Tip:** Knowing if a verb takes a direct object or not will help you use it correctly in a sentence.

1. A storm **destroyed** buildings near the beach.   transitive   intransitive
2. When John left the party, no one **noticed**.   transitive   intransitive
3. Everyone **noticed** Penny when she walked into the room.   transitive   intransitive
4. How does pollution **affect** coral?   transitive   intransitive
5. They **escaped** during the night.   transitive   intransitive
6. Heat **melts** ice and turns it to water.   transitive   intransitive
7. You'll love the way this chocolate **melts** in your mouth.   transitive   intransitive
8. This product may **contain** nuts.   transitive   intransitive

DEVELOPING YOUR READING SKILLS

Topics of Paragraphs

Look at the list of paragraph topics from "Underwater Wonderland" Find the paragraph on each topic in the reading. Write the paragraph number (1–9).

a. colonies of coral polyps   Paragraph ____

b. describing coral polyps   Paragraph ____

c. how coral polyps build reefs   Paragraph ____

d. Marine Protected Areas   Paragraph ____

e. introducing the Great Barrier Reef   Paragraph ____

f. the size of the Great Barrier Reef   Paragraph ____

g. some history of the Great Barrier Reef   Paragraph ____

h. two problems affecting coral worldwide   Paragraph ____

i. two problems that have affected the Great Barrier Reef   Paragraph ____

Clues to Meaning

Noticing Clues to Meaning

Sometimes writers state the meaning of a word in a sentence.

- This sentence from "Underwater Wonderland" explains Marine Protected Areas: "These are parts of the ocean that are like national parks on land."
- This sentence from "The Crab" defines *exoskeleton:* "All crabs have a hard shell, called an exoskeleton."

Writers also have other ways to help the reader understand word meanings. Clues to meaning may be set off by punctuation—parentheses, commas, or dashes—or they may be found in a footnote, an illustration, a caption, or a note in the margin.

Find information in "Underwater Wonderland" that helps you understand the words in this list. Write definitions.

1. coral polyps _____

   _____

2. a tentacle _____

   _____

3. a coral colony _____

   _____

4. species _____

   _____

5. calcium carbonate _____

   _____

6. cyclone _____

   _____

Reading for Details

Are these statements about the reading true or false? If the reading doesn't give the information, check (✓) *It doesn't say.*

	True	False	It doesn't say.
1. The Australian government does not let people enter the Great Barrier Reef Marine Park.			
2. The Great Barrier Reef is made up of both islands and coral reefs.			
3. The Great Barrier Reef has attracted over 1,500 species of fish.			
4. A coral polyp has no eyes, no heart, and no brain.			
5. About 400 species of coral polyps live in the Great Barrier Reef.			
6. It is safe for swimmers to touch the coral.			
7. There are rules about what you can and cannot do in an MPA.			

Main Ideas

Answer the questions using information from the reading.

1. What is special about the Great Barrier Reef?

_____

_____

_____

2. How are coral reefs built?

_____

_____

_____

3. What has been happening to the Great Barrier Reef?

_____

_____

_____

CRITICAL THINKING

Discussion

Talk about these questions in a small group.

1. In paragraph 3, the writer says, "It may be difficult to think of coral polyps as animals." What does the writer mean? Do you agree? Why or why not?

2. On a piece of paper, make a chart like the one below. In the Causes column, list at least four causes of coral reef destruction in the Great Barrier Reef. In the Solutions column, list things that people can do to fix the problem.

Problem	Causes	Solutions
coral reef destruction in the Great Barrier Reef		

3. The reading mentions "human activities" in paragraph 9 and gives the example of commercial fishing. What other kinds of human activities do you think the writer means? What does it mean to say "human activities are controlled?" Tell what controls you think are needed, if any, and why.

4. The writer says, "More MPAs are needed." Is this a fact or an opinion? What support for this idea does the writer give? Does the writer believe that establishing more MPAs will save the coral? Explain your answer.

5. In the first paragraph, the writer made the point that "what is most special about the Great Barrier Reef is what you can see underwater." How does the writer support that point in the reading? Is there enough support to convince you (to get you to agree)? Why or why not?

> **Critical Thinking Tip:** Remember that a fact is something that can be shown to be true. An opinion is something that a person or a group feels or believes but is not true for everyone.

WRITING

A. Use the Target Vocabulary: Choose five target words or phrases from the list on page 130. On a piece of paper, use each word or phrase in a sentence. Then find a partner and read each other's sentences.

B. Practice Writing: Choose a topic and write a paragraph. Then find a partner and read each other's paragraphs.

1. Go online and look up the Seven Wonders of the Natural World. Choose one to write about. Give some important facts about it, and explain why it interests you.

2. For the people of Australia, the Great Barrier Reef is a national treasure. *A national treasure* means something that a country is very proud of and places a high value on. Is there something in your country, something in nature, that you consider a national treasure? Describe it and explain why you chose it.

UNIT 3

Checkpoint

LEARNING OUTCOME

❯ Review and expand on the content
  of Unit 3

LOOK BACK

A. Think About This

Think again about the *Think About This* question on page 95:
What was the topic of the last news report you saw or heard about the ocean?
Do you want to add anything new?

B. Remember the Readings

What do you want to remember most from the readings in Unit 3? For each
chapter, write one sentence about the reading.

Chapter 9: What Does the Ocean Mean to Us?

_____

Chapter 10: The Crab

_____

Chapter 11: Cleaning Up the Ocean

_____

Chapter 12: Underwater Wonderland

_____

REVIEWING VOCABULARY

A. Write the nouns next to their definitions. There are two extra nouns.

activity	coast	emotion	oxygen	pollution
base	effort	nature	point	storm

1. _____ = the area where the land meets the ocean

2. _____ = things that make air, water, soil, etc., dangerously dirty

3. _____ = something that people do, either for fun or to reach a goal

4. _____ = a time of very bad, even violent, weather

5. _____ = a strong human feeling, such as love or hate

6. _____ = the action of trying to do something or the energy spent trying to do it

7. _____ = a gas in the air that all forms of animal and plant life need to live

8. _____ = the lowest or bottom part of something

B. Complete the sentences with phrases from the box. There is one extra phrase.

have in common	keep on	make a difference	makes sense	up to
in all	made sure	make up	puts up with	

1. Earth is the only planet we have, so we should take care of it. Do you

   agree that _____?

2. Those two friends seem so different. I wonder what they

   _____.

3. They are hoping to get _____ ten volunteers. There isn't

   room for any more than ten.

4. The boat on the beach looked very old, so we _____ it would

   float before we got in.

5. There are five named oceans _____: the Atlantic, the Pacific, the Indian, the Southern, and the Arctic.

6. The five named oceans, together with all the named seas, _____ "the ocean."

7. It doesn't matter if we fail on our first try. We'll _____ trying.

8. Oksana shows a lot of patience when tourists complain to her. I couldn't do her job. I don't know how she _____ it.

EXPANDING VOCABULARY

Adverbs

Adverbs have many uses. An adverb can modify, or describe, (1) a verb, (2) an adjective, (3) another adverb, or (4) an entire sentence. An adverb can be one word or a phrase.

1. verb + **adverb**

   *She spoke **calmly**.*
   *They worked **fast**.*

   *He covered the baby **gently**.*
   *You speak English **well**.*

2. **adverb** + adjective

   *You are **exactly** right.*
   *The water was **too** cold.*

   *I'm not **entirely** sure.*
   *They got **violently** seasick.*

3. **adverb** + adverb

   *He can sing **fairly** well.*

   *The situation turned out **rather** badly.*

4. **adverb** + sentence

   ***Basically**, nothing has changed.*
   *He should not have been there **in the first place**.*

Complete the sentences. Use adverbs from the box above. For some sentences, there can be more than one answer.

1. Your situation and mine are _____ different.

2. Please try to answer _____ if any of our customers complain.

3. _____, the coral reef was entirely destroyed.

4. The coastal cleanup is going _____ well.

5. Why is all that plastic in the ocean _____?

A PUZZLE

Complete the sentences with words you studied in Chapters 9–12. Write the words in the puzzle.

ACROSS

1. Coffee, tea, and chocolate all _____ caffeine.

4. My room is always a mess. I need a _____ for keeping it in good order.

6. Computers and cell phones are examples of _____.

8. How does space travel _____ the human body?

10. He likes most vegetables but won't eat _____ ones.

11. I depend on you to _____ me with the latest news.

12. Before you mail the letter, make sure you _____ a stamp.

DOWN

2. At night, the outdoor lights _____ flying insects.

3. I use my phone or my computer to _____ to the Internet.

5. Plastic usually floats on the _____ of the ocean.

7. The technology wasn't working well, so the team is trying to

_____ something better.

9. Pollution is bad for the _____—and for us!

BUILDING DICTIONARY SKILLS

A. Look at the two entries for *heat* and answer the questions below.

> **heat¹** /hit/ *n.* **1** [U] warmth or the quality of being hot: *heat from the sun* **2** [U] very hot weather: *I can't work in this heat.* **3** [U] the system that keeps a place warm, or the warmth from this system: *Let's turn the heat on.* **4** [C] one of the parts of a sports competition from which the winner goes on to the next part
>
> **heat²** *v.* [T] make something warm or hot: *I'll heat some soup for lunch.* **heat up** *phr. v.* **1** [T/I] to make (something) or become warm or hot: *The car takes time to heat up./heat it up in the microwave* **2** if a situation heats up, it becomes dangerous or full of problems

1. Which parts of speech can *heat* be? Circle your answers.

    noun   verb   adjective   adverb

2. How many meanings for *heat* does this dictionary give? ____

3. Does the verb *heat* take a direct object?   YES   NO   SOMETIMES

B. Look at this entry for the noun *wave*. Write the number of the meaning used in each sentence below.

____ a. The child gave her mother a wave and ran to join her friends.

____ b. The waves are too big for people to swim today.

____ c. When I heard the news, I felt a wave of fear come over me.

____ d. Light and sound move in waves.

> **wave¹** /weɪv/ *n* [C] **1** an area of raised water that moves across the surface of the ocean or another large area of water: *waves breaking on the beach* **2** a sudden increase in a particular emotion, activity, number, etc.: *a recent crime wave | a wave of nostalgia for his childhood | a sudden wave of nausea | a great wave of immigrants from Eastern Europe* **3** the movement you make when you wave your hand: *She left with a wave of her hand.* **4** a part of your hair that curls slightly: *a wave in her hair* **5** the form in which some types of energy move: *light/sound/radio waves* **6 make waves** *informal* to cause problems: *We have a job to finish, so don't make waves, OK?*

142 will be a blank page

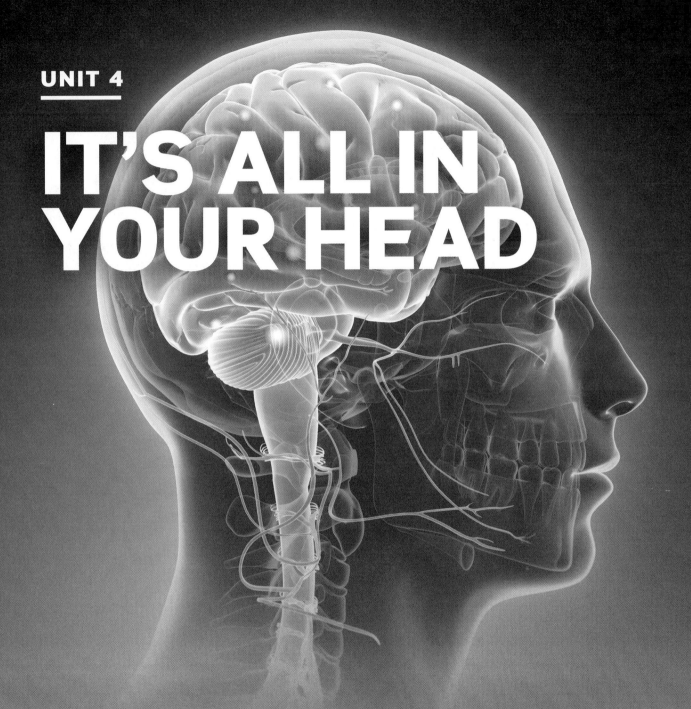

UNIT 4

IT'S ALL IN YOUR HEAD

THINK ABOUT THIS

Do you think these sentences are true or false? Check ✔ your answers.

	TRUE	FALSE
1. Your brain weighs about three pounds (1.36 kg).	☐	☐
2. Different parts of your brain serve different purposes.	☐	☐
3. Different foods affect your brain in different ways.	☐	☐
4. Your brain uses 20–30% of the energy you get from your food.	☐	☐
5. Your brain is busy working even when you sleep.	☐	☐

CHAPTER 13

Food for Thought

Morning coffee

GETTING READY TO READ

Talk about these questions with your class.

1. How many people in the class drink:

   _____ coffee

   _____ tea

   _____ soda

   _____ energy drinks

2. The drinks in the list usually contain caffeine.[1] Some of them can also be decaf (that is, decaffeinated, or caffeine free). How many people in the class drink decaf coffee, tea, or soda?

3. When and why do people like drinks with caffeine?

[1] *caffeine* = a substance (in coffee, tea, and some other drinks) that makes your brain feel more awake

READING

Read to Find Out: What change in human history may have helped the brain grow larger?

Look at the words and definitions next to the reading. Then read without stopping.

Food for Thought

1   The foods you eat supply your body with energy. Your body needs energy to move, breathe, and even to sleep. One part of your body uses a surprising **amount** of energy. It's surprising because this part of your body is small—only 2 to 3 percent of your total **weight**—but it uses 20 to 30 percent of the energy from your food. Can you guess what it is? It's your brain.

2   No doubt you know that drugs affect the brain, but did you know that food affects it, too? Different types of food affect the brain in different ways. Sometimes we can feel the changes that food makes in our brains. For example, most people can feel a change almost **immediately** after drinking coffee. The caffeine in coffee makes people feel mentally sharper[1] and more awake. After a cup of coffee, a person can think and make decisions more quickly.

3   Other foods affect the brain in ways that we cannot feel, so we aren't aware of the effects. We do not **realize** how these foods **influence** us. However, everything we eat matters. Our food affects how smart we are, how well we remember things, and how long we can concentrate.[2] For example, researchers have found that:

- Eating breakfast makes students do better on tests.
- Spinach, berries, and other colorful fruits and vegetables help keep older brains from slowing down.
- Eating large amounts of animal fat (in meat and cheese, for example) makes learning more difficult.
- Fish really is "brain food." Many people have long believed that eating fish was good for the brain, and now scientists are finding that this is true.

4   For millions of years, the brains of early human beings[3] stayed the same size. They weighed only about one pound (400 to 500 grams). Then, during the last million years **or so**, there was a big **increase** in brain size, with the human brain growing to about three pounds on average. This increase in brain size **meant** an increase in brainpower. With bigger, more **powerful**, more **advanced** brains, human beings became smart enough to build boats and invent written languages. They developed forms of music and began to **create** works of art.[4]

[1] *mentally sharper* = able to think and understand more quickly

[2] *concentrate* = think carefully

[3] *early human beings* = the first people who lived

[4] *works of art* = the things that artists make

5   Some scientists say that the big change in the size of the human brain happened after people started to eat fish and other kinds of seafood. Seafood contains a certain kind of fat, known as omega-3 fat. **According to** these scientists, omega-3 fat caused the increase in brain size. Today, brain scientists in general agree: This fat is still important for healthy brains, and most of us are not getting enough of it.

6   Did you realize that your brain is always changing, **no matter** how old you are? The foods you eat affect how your brain grows, how well you learn, and how well you remember things. Maybe you have never thought about how you **feed** your brain. **Luckily**, it's never too late to start feeding it well.

Quick Comprehension Check

A. Read these sentences **about the reading**. Circle T (true) or F (false). On the line, write the number of the paragraph with the answer.

1. Children's brains go through changes, but adult brains don't.   T   F   _____

2. Your brain is small but uses a lot of energy.   T   F   _____

3. The foods you eat affect the way your brain works.   T   F   _____

4. When a food causes changes in your brain, you can always feel it.   T   F   _____

5. Maybe eating fish helped make the human brain bigger.   T   F   _____

6. All kinds of fat are bad for you.   T   F   _____

B. Work with your class. Share your answers from part A. Go back to the reading to find the reason why a statement is true or false. Correct the false statements.

EXPLORING VOCABULARY

Thinking about the Target Vocabulary

A. Look at the chart with the target vocabulary. Three nouns and five verbs are missing. Scan the reading to find them, and add them to the correct places in the chart. Write the singular form of any plural noun. Write the base form of each verb.

¶	Nouns	Verbs	Adjectives	Other
1				
2				immediately
3				
4				or so
			powerful	
			advanced	
5				according to
6				no matter
				luckily

B. Which target words or phrases are new to you? Circle them in the chart. Then find them in the reading. Look at the context. Can you guess the meaning?

Using the Target Vocabulary

A. These sentences are **about the reading**. Complete them with the words and phrases in the box.

according to	feeding	influence	meant	realize
advanced	immediately	luckily	no matter	weight

1. Your brain is not very heavy. It is only 2 to 3 percent of your total body

   _____.

2. Sometimes a drug or food affects the brain quickly and people feel the

   difference very soon. They feel a change _____.

3. Many people aren't aware that food affects the brain. They don't

   _____, or understand, that this is true.

4. When foods affect the brain, they cause changes in how we think and

   act. However, we aren't always aware of this. We don't always realize

   how these foods _____ us.

5. When the human brain got bigger, that change led to a certain result. A

   bigger brain _____ more brainpower.

6. As the human brain grew and became more powerful, it developed to a

   higher stage. Because it became more _____, people were

   able to produce art, music, and written languages.

7. Some scientists say that eating seafood had an important effect on the

   human brain. _____ these scientists, seafood helped the

   human brain to grow.

8. Your brain is always changing. This is true for young and old.

   _____ your age, your brain continues to change.

9. When you eat foods that are good for your brain, you are

   _____ your brain well.

10. Maybe you never thought about eating "brain food" before, but there

    is good news: you can do something about it now. _____,

    it's not too late to start.

Reading Tip:
Luckily often shows the writer's opinion. It's often used to introduce information the writer considers good news.

B. These sentences use the target words and phrases **in new contexts**.
Complete them with the words and phrases in the box.

according to	fed	influence	meant	realized
advanced	immediately	luckily	no matter	weight

1. There was a car accident there today. _____, no one was

   hurt.

2. Fruit is often sold by _____—you pay by the pound or

   kilogram.

3. We are both studying Spanish, but I'm a beginner and he's in an

   _____ class.

4. The president has the power to _____ people and events and to affect the future of the country.

5. He needed medical care _____, so we rushed him to the hospital.

6. She was already in bed for the night when I called. I suddenly _____ how late it was and said I was sorry about calling at that hour.

7. We took the children to the park and _____ bread to the ducks and other birds.

8. The snowstorm brought a foot of snow, and that _____ that several airports had to close.

9. Paolo will keep on running, _____ how tired he gets, until he finishes the race.

10. _____ the newspaper, the point of the new state law is to attract more businesses to the state.

> **Vocabulary Tip:**
> *Influence* can be a noun or a verb. The preposition *on* (+ someone or something) often follows the noun: *His parents thought his friends were a bad influence on him.*

> **Vocabulary Tip:**
> The verb *mean* has several meanings. It's often used to give definitions, but in sentence 8, it means "have a certain result."

C. Read each definition and look at the paragraph number. Look back at the reading on pages 145–146 to find the **boldfaced** word or phrase to match the definition. Copy it in the chart.

Definition	Paragraph	Target Word or Phrase
1. how much of something there is	1	
2. a phrase used when you cannot give an exact number or amount	4	
3. a change to a higher number or larger amount	4	
4. having a lot of ability to control or influence things	4	
5. invent, design, or develop something new	4	

Building on the Vocabulary

> **Collocations: *Amount***
>
> Certain adjectives go with the noun *amount*.
> - Use *large* + *amount* but not ~~big~~ *amount*
>   *He never carries* large amounts *of money.*
> - Use *small* + *amount* but not ~~little~~ *amount*
>   *I eat chocolate* in small amounts.
>
> Certain nouns can follow *amount of*.
> - Use *amount* + *of* + a noncount noun (such as *energy*, *time*, *money*, or *work*).
>   *The manager discovered that a* large amount of money *was missing.*

A. Circle the correct word.

1. The volunteers picked up (big / large) amounts of trash.

2. I like sugar in my tea, but only a (little / small) amount.

3. What's the average amount of (time / minutes) you end up waiting for a bus to school in the morning?

B. Write two sentences with *amount*.

1. _____

   _____

2. _____

   _____

Writing Tip:
Remember: collocations are words that go together. Some words are often found together while other words cannot be used together.

DEVELOPING YOUR READING SKILLS

Scanning

Read these statements about "Food for Thought." Scan the reading for the information you need to complete them. Answers inside quotation marks (" ") must match the words in the reading exactly.

1. The foods you eat give your body _____.

2. The brain makes up only _____ percent of your body's total weight.

3. The brain uses _____ percent of the energy from your food.

4. The _____ in coffee makes people feel more awake.

5. Scientists have found that:

   a. "Eating breakfast _____."

   b. "_____" are good for older brains.

   c. "Eating large amounts of animal fat _____

      _____."

   d. "_____ really is 'brain food.'"

6. Early human brains grew from about _____ to about

   _____.

7. Some scientists say the human brain grew because of the _____

   in seafood.

8. With bigger, more powerful brains, human beings were able to build

   _____, invent _____, and create _____.

Main Ideas

A. Complete the main idea of "Food for Thought."

The foods you eat affect how _____

_____

_____.

B. What is the main idea of paragraph 1 in "Food for Thought"? Write one or two sentences.

_____

_____

_____

C. What is the main idea of paragraph 6 in "Food for Thought"? Write one or two sentences.

_____

_____

_____

Making Inferences

Make inferences to answer the questions. Write complete sentences.

1. What advice does the reading give students about which foods to eat?

   _____

   _____

2. What advice does the reading give people in general about which foods to eat?

   _____

   _____

3. According to the reading, what do scientists disagree on?

   _____

   _____

CRITICAL THINKING

Discussion

Talk about these questions in a small group.

1. In paragraph 3, find the phrase "brain food." What does it mean? The writer tells what "many people" have believed for a long time. Are you one of the many people who share that belief? Are there other foods that people in your culture speak of as "brain food"?

2. Do scientists all agree that eating seafood led to the increase in the size of the human brain? Do scientists all agree that people should eat omega-3 fat? Underline the parts of the reading that support your answers.

3. What information about omega-3 fat is missing from the reading? Write two questions about it. How would you find the answers to your questions?

4. In paragraph 6, the writer uses "Luckily." Whose good luck is the writer talking about? How and why are they lucky?

5. According to the reading, what should we eat—and not eat—to help our brains? How much would you change the way you eat to make yourself smarter? Tell one change you would be ready to make and one change you would not make. Explain your answers.

WRITING

A. Use the Target Vocabulary: Choose five target words or phrases from the list on page 147. On a piece of paper, use each word or phrase in a sentence. Underline the target vocabulary. Then find a partner and read each other's sentences.

B. Practice Writing: Choose one of these topics and write a paragraph about it. Then find a partner and read each other's paragraphs.

1. Write about something you like to eat or drink. When do you usually have it? How does it affect you? Do you think it's good or bad for you? Why? Has the information in the reading influenced your thinking about it?

2. The reading suggests one way of taking care of your brain— feeding it well. What else do you think a person can do to take care of their brain? Explain where your information and understanding about the brain comes from.

> **Writing Tip:** You can introduce a sentence about your own beliefs with the phrase "In my opinion." Do not use "According to me" or "According to my opinion." These phrases are not correct.

CHAPTER 14

Your Memory At Work

Trying to remember…

GETTING READY TO READ

Talk about these questions with a partner.

1. Look at the things in the list. Which ones are usually easy for you to remember? Which ones are hard?

   people's names   colors   words to songs

   people's faces   music   information from classes

   numbers   new vocabulary in English   other: _____

2. When you MUST remember something, what do you do? How do you help yourself remember it?

READING

Read to Find Out: What can you do to help yourself remember important information?

Look at the picture, words, and definitions next to the reading. Then read without stopping.

Your Memory at Work

1   You have two basic types of **memory**: short-**term** memory and long-term memory. Things you see or hear first enter your short-term memory. Very little of this information then passes on into your long-term memory. Does this mean you have a bad memory? Not at all.

2   Your short-term memory has a certain job to do. Its job is to **store** information for a few seconds only. You use your short-term memory when you **look up** a phone number, call it, and then forget it. You remember the number just long enough to use it, and then it disappears from your memory. That's really a good thing. **Imagine** if your memory held every number, face, and word you ever knew! Your brain would hold a mountain of trivia.[1]

[1] *trivia =
unimportant or
useless details*

3   Of course, we need to remember some information longer, so it has to pass from short-term to long-term memory. Sometimes we tell ourselves to remember: "OK, don't forget: 555-1212, 555-1212… " But usually, we don't even think about it. Our brain makes the decision for us. It decides to store the information or let it go.

4   The brain seems to make the decision by asking two questions:

   • Does the new information affect our emotions? Does it make us happy, sad, angry, or excited?

   • Does the new information **concern** something we already know, so our brain can store it with information that is already there?

An answer of "yes" to one or both of these questions sends the new information into long-term memory. That means the brain creates new **connections** among brain cells.[2] These connections form in a **region** of the brain called the cerebral cortex.[3] It's the largest part of the brain.

[2] *cell = in any
living thing, the
smallest part
that can live by
itself*

5   After a piece of information enters your long-term memory, how do you get it back? Sometimes your brain may seem like a deep, dark **closet**. You open the door to look for something—you are sure it's in there somewhere—but you cannot find it. Maybe the information is no longer there. Information disappears when connections among brain cells become **weak**. They get weak if time passes and the connections are not used. That is why it's good to **review** your **notes** from a **lecture** soon after the class. Do not wait too long to "look in the closet."

[3] *the cerebral
cortex*

6   To keep the memory of something strong, think of it often. For example, look at those lecture notes the next day and the day after that, too. Then wait a few days and review them again. Every time you think about something, the connections in the brain get stronger. Then it's easier to remember the information when you need it.

7   **Unfortunately**, this advice **applies** only to certain kinds of things that you try to remember. It won't help when you are trying to remember a name that's on the tip of your tongue. A "tip of the tongue" experience is the feeling that you're about to remember a word but it just won't come out. These experiences are common among older adults, but everyone has them. College students, on average, have one or two a week.

8   This advice also won't help you remember something that just never made it[4] from short-term to long-term memory. No matter how hard you try, you won't find it in your memory. So you'll need some other strategy[5] to help you figure out where you left your keys.

[4] *made it =* managed to arrive

[5] *strategy =* plans and skills used to reach a goal

Quick Comprehension Check

A. Read these sentences **about the reading**. Circle T (true) or F (false). On the line, write the number of the paragraph with the answer.

1. People have two basic types of memory.   T   F   _____

2. Your short-term memory holds information for just a few days.   T   F   _____

3. All information should go to your long-term memory.   T   F   _____

4. Information in long-term memory will always be there.   T   F   _____

5. There are things you can do to help your memory.   T   F   _____

6. We usually remember information that affects how we feel.   T   F   _____

B. Work with your class. Share your answers from part A. Go back to the reading to find the reason why a statement is true or false. Correct the false statements.

EXPLORING VOCABULARY

Thinking about the Target Vocabulary

A. Look at the chart with the target vocabulary. Six verbs, one adjective, and one adverb are missing. Scan the reading to find them, and add them to the correct places in the chart. Write the base form of each verb.

¶	Nouns	Verbs	Adjectives	Other
1	memory			
	term			
2				
4				
	connection			
	region			
5	closet			
	notes			
	lecture			
7				

> **Vocabulary Tip:** *Notes* is always plural when it means "information a student writes down during a lesson, from a book, etc."

B. Which target words or phrases are new to you? Circle them in the chart. Then find them in the reading. Look at the context. Can you guess the meaning?

Using the Target Vocabulary

A. These sentences are **about the reading**. What is the meaning of each **boldfaced** word? Circle a, b, or c.

1. People have two basic types of **memory**. *Memory* means the ability to

   a. create.   b. float.   c. remember.

2. The job of your short-term memory is to **store** information for just a few seconds. When you store something, you

  a. keep it somewhere until it's needed.   b. increase it.   c. change your mind about it.

3. The reading asks you to **imagine** a situation: Imagine holding in memory every number, face, and word you ever knew in your entire life. *Imagine* means

  a. picture something in your mind.   b. volunteer to help with something.   c. put up with something.

4. It is easier to remember new facts or ideas when they **concern** something we already know. *Concern something* means

  a. be about that topic.   b. destroy that thing.   c. end up in that situation.

5. New **connections** form among brain cells when we learn something new. *Connections* means places where

  a. nothing happens.   b. things come together.   c. something stops.

6. To hold information in memory, the brain creates connections in the cerebral cortex. The cerebral cortex is a **region** of the brain. A region is

  a. a talent.   b. a stage.   c. an area.

7. We forget things when connections among brain cells get **weak**. *Weak* means

  a. sharp.   b. not strong.   c. secure.

8. Students are wise to review their **notes** soon after a class. Their notes are

  a. their grades.   b. information they write down in class.   c. their favorite music.

9. **Unfortunately**, some things that you can do to help your memory won't help you in every case. Use *unfortunately* to introduce information that is

  a. encouraging.   b. amazing.   c. disappointing.

> **Vocabulary Tip:**
> *Unfortunately* and *luckily* are antonyms (words with opposite meanings).

10. The advice in the reading **applies** in some situations but not others. When a rule, a law, or a piece of advice applies to someone, it

  a. affects or concerns them.   b. attacks them.   c. surprises them.

B. These sentences use the target words and phrases **in new contexts**. Complete them with the words in the box.

apply	connection	memory	region	unfortunately
concerns	imagine	notes	stored	weak

1. Students often take _____ in class about things they want to remember.

Writing Tip: The verb *take*, not *write*, is used with *notes*.

2. Do you ever _____ yourself traveling into space and visiting other planets?

3. People in some places have to pay a sales tax on the things they buy, but sometimes the sales tax does not _____ to sales of food or medicine.

4. Mike lives in a _____ where they get a lot of snow.

5. _____, Elsa wasn't able to get an interview for the job she wanted.

6. Some foods, like fresh milk, must be _____ at cold temperatures.

7. If it is easy for you to remember things, then you can say you have a good _____.

8. A report in today's newspaper _____ a new effort to clean up ocean pollution.

9. Being sick for so long made Jeff lose a lot of weight and feel _____.

Vocabulary Tip: The verb *concern* is related to the preposition *concerning*, meaning "about, relating to:" *Customers had questions concerning the new software.*

10. When one fact, idea, or event affects another, we can say there is a _____ between them.

C. Read each definition and look at the paragraph number. Look back at the reading on pages 155–156 to find the **boldfaced** word or phrase to match the definition. Copy it in the chart.

Definition	Paragraph	Target Word
1. a certain amount of time	1	
2. try to find (information in a book, online, etc.)	2	
3. an area where people hang clothes or store things (behind a door in a wall)	5	
4. look at or read again and study	5	
5. a long talk on one subject, given to a group of people, often students	5	

Writing Tip: After *lecture* (as a noun or a verb), use the preposition *on* + a topic: *He gave a lecture on climate change. She lectures on the brain.*

Building on the Vocabulary

Word Grammar: Meanings and Uses of *Memory*

Memory has several meanings other than the ability to remember things.

memory [C, usually plural] something you remember from the past: *I have happy memories from my last vacation.*

memory [C,U] the part of a computer where information can be stored or the amount of space available for storing information on a computer: *How much memory does this computer have?*

in memory of if something is done in memory of someone, it is done to make people remember the person after he or she has died: *Airports, roads, and buildings are sometimes named in memory of presidents.*

Write three sentences using **memory, memories,** and **in memory of.**

1. _____

2. _____

3. _____

DEVELOPING YOUR READING SKILLS

Topics of Paragraphs

Look at the list of paragraph topics from "Your Memory at Work." Find the paragraph on each topic in the reading. Write the paragraph number (1–8).

a. how the brain deals with new information   Paragraph ____

b. types of memory   Paragraph ____

c. connections among brain cells growing weak   Paragraph ____

d. building strong connections among brain cells   Paragraph ____

e. what short-term memory does   Paragraph ____

f. "tip of the tongue" experiences   Paragraph ____

g. information you won't find in your memory   Paragraph ____

h. information passing from short-term to long-term memory   Paragraph ____

Main Ideas

A. Which sentence gives the main idea of the reading? Check ☑ your answer.

☐ 1. Understanding how memory works can help you remember important information.

2. If information enters your long-term memory, you will always remember it.

3. When you try to remember something, look in both your short-term and long-term memories.

B. Which sentence gives the main idea of paragraph 5? Check ☑ your answer.

1. Put memories in order in your mind so that "the closet" of your brain is not a mess.

2. Information disappears from long-term memory if you do not think about it often enough.

3. Over time, your ability to remember things grows weaker because you are growing older.

Summarizing

Complete the summary of "Your Memory at Work." Write one or more words on each line.

The two basic types of memory are ___short-term memory___ and
(1)

_____. Information stays in short-term memory for
(2)

_____. Then, if it is not important, the information
(3)

_____. When information is important to
(4)

remember, it has to enter _____. That is where new
(5)

_____ are formed among brain cells. You make them
(6)

stronger—so you remember the information more easily--each time that you

_____ the information.
(7)

CRITICAL THINKING

Discussion

Talk about these questions in a small group.

1. What does "that" mean in "That's really a good thing" (paragraph 2)? Why does the writer say it is a good thing? Do you agree? Explain your answer.

Critical Thinking Tip:
Sometimes writers give their opinion openly; sometimes you can infer it. In either case, ask yourself, "Do I agree? Why or why not?"

2. Read these three situations, and decide if the information described would be stored in your long-term memory or not, based on the information in the reading.

   a. You have just read a news story about someone you knew years ago. You found the story both surprising and exciting. Will you probably remember it to tell a friend about it a few days later? What information in the reading supports your answer?

   b. You and a friend are sitting together. You are reading a news story on an English website. You find a word you don't know, and you ask your friend what it means. Your friend gives you a translation of the word, and you go back to reading. You don't see that word again. A week later, you are writing a paragraph in English, and you want to use that word. Do you think you'll remember it? What information in the reading supports your answer?

   c. You hear a new song on the radio that you like. You immediately go online, find the song, read the words to it, and listen to it again. Later, you tell a friend about the song and listen to it together. Before you fall asleep that night, you think about it. Will you be able to sing any of the song or remember the words to it the next day? What information in the reading supports your answer?

3. In paragraph 5, what does the writer compare your brain to? How are the two things alike? What do you think is the writer's purpose in making this comparison?

4. The reading says that the more you review information, the better you remember it. According to the reading, *why* is this true? Do you find this to be true? What has your experience been?

> **Reading Tip:** Writers sometimes compare a new idea to something that is well-known to the reader. Thinking about how the two things are alike will help you understand the new idea.

WRITING

A. Use the Target Vocabulary: Choose five target words or phrases from the list on page 157. On a piece of paper, use each word or phrase in a sentence. Underline the target vocabulary. Then find a partner and read each other's sentences.

B. Practice Writing: Choose one of these topics and write a paragraph about it. Then find a partner and read each other's paragraphs.

   1. What helps you remember new words in English? Describe what you do to make sure you do not forget the words you learn. Tell what is most helpful.

   2. Most people cannot remember anything from their lives before the age of three or four. What are your earliest memories? Why do you think you remember those things?

CHAPTER 15

Sleep and the Brain

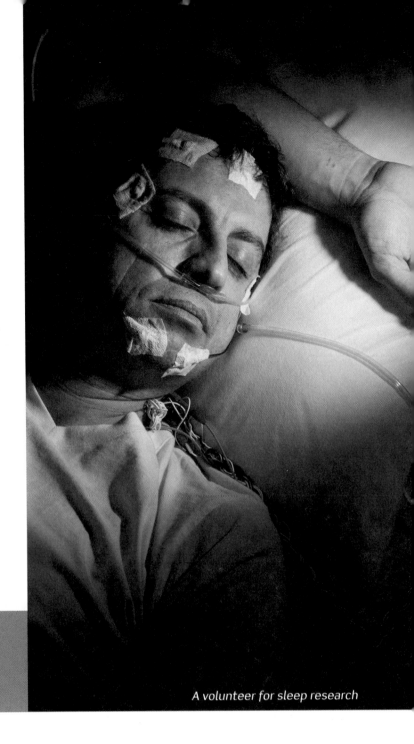

A volunteer for sleep research

LEARNING OUTCOME

❯ Learn about what happens in your brain as you sleep

GETTING READY TO READ

Talk about these questions with a partner.

1. How many hours of sleep do you usually get? Would you like to sleep more? Less? Explain why.

2. Do you think these statements are true or false? Why?

    a. Our brains are completely at rest (they "turn off") when we sleep.

    b. We spend only 2 to 4 percent of a night's sleep time dreaming.

    c. Sleeping during the day can be good for your brain.

Read to Find Out: What does the writer suggest you do?

Look at the picture, words, and definitions next to the reading. Then read without stopping.

Sleep and the Brain

1   Human beings, like all mammals,[1] need sleep. Adults need an average of 7.5 hours a night. However, the average amount of sleep might not be right for you, just as the average-size shoe might not be right for your foot. The usual sleep **schedule—that is**, doing all your sleeping at night—might not be right for you either. Getting some sleep during the day may be exactly what your brain needs.

[1] *mammals = animals that get milk from their mother when young*

2   We may not all need the same amount of sleep or the same sleep schedule, but everyone needs the same two types of sleep. Our sleep is **divided** between REM sleep and NREM sleep (which you can **pronounce** "en-rem" or "non-rem"):

   • *REM* comes from the words "rapid eye movement." During this type of sleep, your eyes move quickly. This eye movement shows that your brain is very **active** and you're dreaming. You spend about 20 percent of the night in REM sleep.

   • *NREM* means "non-REM," or no eye movement. This type of sleep has four stages.

3   When you fall asleep, you enter Stage 1 of NREM sleep. This is a light sleep, so a noise could easily wake you up. After several minutes, you enter Stage 2. It's not so easy to wake you up from this type of sleep. Stages 3 and 4 are **periods** of deep sleep. You breathe slowly, your muscles[2] relax, your heart **rate** slows, and your brain becomes less active.

[2] *muscles*

4   You experience both REM and NREM sleep when you go through a sleep cycle. A cycle is a group of events that happens again and again, like the cycle of **seasons** that happens each year. A sleep cycle takes you from light sleep to deep sleep and back again. It **includes** the four

Sleep Cycles

Time, hrs	0	1	2	3	4	5	6	7	8
Awake									
REM			5 min		10 min		15 min		30-60 min
Stage 1									
Stage 2									
Stage 3									
Stage 4									

stages of NREM sleep, then a short period of REM sleep, and finally a return to light, NREM sleep. At night, most people go through a **series** of four to six sleep cycles.

5   It's good to understand sleep cycles and the stages of NREM sleep if you ever take **naps** during the day. A nap of 20 to 45 minutes will mean getting mostly Stage 2 sleep. It will mean sharper motor skills[3] and a better ability to **focus** your mind and **pay attention**. That is exactly what most people hope for when they take a nap.

6   A longer nap may not do you as much good.[4] It may mean that you enter the deep sleep of Stage 3 or 4. If your alarm[5] wakes you during deep sleep, you will wake up unable to think clearly. You will probably feel more tired than you did before your nap, and it can take 30 minutes or more to **get over** this feeling.

7   However, a longer nap can do you good if it covers a full sleep cycle. That takes 90 to 120 minutes. If your alarm wakes you up at the end of a full sleep cycle, you will be coming out of a light sleep, and your brain will have all the advantages[6] of a good rest. Those good effects can last for up to 10 hours.

8   If you live a busy life, you probably do not always get a full night's sleep. Not getting enough sleep can mean you forget words, you have trouble learning, and you react[7] more slowly. You can probably think of other effects of too little sleep. So consider taking a nap, for the good of your brain, and think about sleep stages if you **set** an alarm.

[3] *motor skills* = skills that depend on the body's nerves and muscles

[4] *do you good* = make you feel better

[5] *alarm* = a clock or other device that makes a loud sound at a planned time

[6] *advantages* = things that help you do better and be more successful

[7] *react* = feel or do something because of something that just happened

Quick Comprehension Check

A. Read these sentences **about the reading**. Circle T (true) or F (false). On the line, write the number of the paragraph with the answer.

1. All adults need the same amount of sleep each night.   T   F   _____

2. We experience two basic types of sleep.   T   F   _____

3. Your eyes move during REM sleep.   T   F   _____

4. During REM sleep, you dream.   T   F   _____

5. During REM sleep, you go through several stages.   T   F   _____

6. Sleep stages affect how you feel when you wake up.   T   F   _____

B. Work with your class. Share your answers from part A. Go back to the reading to find the reason why a statement is true or false. Correct the false statements.

EXPLORING VOCABULARY

Thinking about the Target Vocabulary

A. Look at the chart with the target vocabulary. Six nouns and one adjective are missing. Scan the reading to find them, and add them to the correct places in the chart. Write the singular form of any plural noun.

¶	Nouns	Verbs	Adjectives	Other
1				
				that is
2		divide		
		pronounce		
3				
4				
		include		
5				
		focus		
				pay attention
6		get over		
8		set		

> **Vocabulary Tip:** *Series* is a count noun. The singular and plural forms are the same. It is usually singular: *a series of events.*

B. Which target words or phrases are new to you? Circle them in the chart. Then find them in the reading. Look at the context. Can you guess the meaning?

Using the Target Vocabulary

A. These sentences are **about the reading**. Complete them with the words and phrases in the box.

divided	get over	pay attention	schedule	set
focus	includes	rate	series	that is

1. Most people have a plan for when they will go to bed and when they will get up. They usually sleep at night. That is their sleep _____.

2. The usual sleep schedule (7 to 8 hours of sleep at night) isn't right for everyone. _____, for some people, it might be better to sleep for a different number of hours or during a different part of the day.

3. We spend part of the night in REM sleep and part in NREM sleep. Our sleep is _____ between these two types of sleep.

> **Writing Tip:** Use *that is* to introduce another way to say something or add details. In item 2, *that is* introduces an explanation of why the usual sleep schedule isn't right for everyone.

4. Your heart _____ tells how fast your heart is working. For example, it may beat 60 or 70 times a minute.

5. REM sleep and NREM sleep are both part of a sleep cycle. A sleep cycle _____ both types of sleep.

6. During the night, you go through four to six sleep cycles. They happen one after another: the first cycle, then the second, then the third, and so on. This is a _____ of sleep cycles.

7. When you need to think about one thing and one thing only, you have to _____ on that one thing.

> **Vocabulary Tip:** *Focus on* and *pay attention to* are very close in meaning, but notice the different prepositions, *on* and *to*, that follow them.

8. Feeling well-rested helps when you need to watch, think about, or listen to someone or something very carefully. It is harder to _____ to things when you are tired.

9. Sometimes you wake up from a nap feeling terrible, and you can't think clearly. You won't feel completely awake, and it takes time to _____ this feeling.

10. When you _____ an alarm clock, you do something to it so that it will make a loud sound at the time you want.

B. These sentences use the target words and phrases **in new contexts**. Complete them with the words and phrases in the box.

divided	get over	paid no attention	schedule	set
focus	included	rates	series	that is

1. One hundred _____ by two is fifty.

2. It takes me a week to ten days to _____ a cold.

3. *Superman—The Movie* was the first in a long _____ of Superman movies.

> **Vocabulary Tip:** Use *get over* (something) to mean "get back to feeling well." You can get over a sickness, an injury, or a disappointment.

4. We looked at the bus _____ to find out when the next bus would come.

5. The traffic light turned red, but the driver _____. He just kept going.

6. There was a lot of noise outside the classroom, making it hard for the students to _____ on their work.

> **Vocabulary Tip:** Use *set* + a clock or other machine, meaning to get it ready to work in the way you want. This verb has many other meanings, too. See your dictionary for more information.

7. I turned on the oven and _____ it to a temperature of 350 degrees.

8. Children learn at different _____. Some learn quickly, others more slowly.

9. My class _____ four students from South America. Two of my classmates were Colombian, and two were from Brazil.

10. People say "Money is the root of all evil." _____, the love of money causes all the problems in the world.

C. Read the sentences. Guess the meaning of the **boldfaced** target words from the context. Match them with their definitions.

a. How do you **pronounce** your last name?

b. Each **period** at the high school is fifty minutes long.

c. Dad sometimes takes a **nap** in the big chair in front of the TV.

d. Canada has four **seasons**: spring, summer, fall, and winter.

e. Some animals sleep during the day and are **active** at night.

Target Word	Definition
1. _____	= always busy doing things
2. _____	= an amount of time
3. _____	= a short period of sleep during the day
4. _____	= say the sound of a letter or word the correct way
5. _____	= one of the main periods that a year is divided into, with each period having a certain type of weather

Building on the Vocabulary

Collocations: Verb + Noun Pairs

Certain verbs form collocations with certain nouns. That is, they are often used together, while other verbs *cannot* be used with that noun, even if those verbs have basically the same meaning. Notice the verb + noun pairs in these sentences.

*After lunch, the children **took naps**.*

*During lectures, students **take notes**.*

*Please **make an effort** to be on time.*

*It **takes** a lot of **effort** to learn a language.*

*A scientist will **give a lecture** on the brain.*

*Did the medicine **have any effect** on the patient?*

*Please **pay attention**!*

Circle the correct verb to complete the sentence.

1. He (made/did) an effort to get over his anger.

2. I'd like to (do/take) a nap, but I don't have time.

3. They should stop talking and (give/pay) attention.

4. Who is (giving/speaking) the lecture?

5. Some students (take/write) good notes in class.

6. The sales tax (made/had) no effect on people's spending.

DEVELOPING YOUR READING SKILLS

Understanding Text Features

> ### Line Graphs
>
> A **line graph**, or line chart, is a good way to show the way that facts change over time. A line graph usually has a title at the top. Read the labels at the left and on the bottom to help you understand the facts presented in the graph.

Look at the line graph on page 164. Answer the questions based on the graph.

1. One hour after falling asleep, what sleep stage is the person in?

   _____

2. At the end of the first sleep cycle, how many minutes does the person

   spend in REM sleep? _____

3. What is one difference between the third sleep cycle and the first two?

   _____

4. When does the person have their longest period of dreaming?

   _____

5. How many sleep cycles are shown in the graph? _____

6. How many minutes does the graph show a person spends in REM sleep

   during the night? _____

> **Critical Thinking Tip:** Remember that you can use text features, such as the line graph in "Sleep and the Brain," to help you understand what you read.

Reading for Details

Are these statements about the reading true or false? If the reading doesn't give the information, check (✓) *It doesn't say.*

	True	False	It doesn't say.
1. The average person needs 7.5 hours of sleep a night.			
2. The two basic types of sleep are REM and NREM sleep.			
3. People's eyes move quickly during NREM sleep.			
4. Most people never remember any dreams.			
5. Stage 1 sleep is very light.			
6. People spend about half the night in Stage 2 sleep.			

	True	False	It doesn't say.
7. People dream the most during deep sleep.			
8. A nap of 20 to 45 minutes usually helps the brain work better.			
9. A longer nap always makes you feel better than a short nap.			
10. Sleeping too many hours a day has bad effects on people.			

Cause and Effect

Use information from the reading to complete the chart. Read the causes and add the effects.

CAUSE		EFFECT
1. dreaming while you sleep	→	rapid eye movements
2. a nap of 20 to 45 minutes	→	
3. waking up from Stage 3 or 4 sleep	→	
4. a nap that lasts a full sleep cycle	→	
5. not getting enough sleep	→	

Summarizing

Complete this summary of "Sleep and the Brain." Write one or more words on each line.

People need different amounts of _____, but everyone
                                         (1)

needs the same _____: REM and NREM sleep. We dream
                     (2)

during _____ and our _____ move quickly.
          (3)   (4)

During NREM sleep, we go through four _____, from light
                                 (5)

sleep to deep sleep. Understanding sleep can help you plan a good

_____. A nap can_____, or it can make you
     (6)   (7)

feel worse.

CRITICAL THINKING

Discussion

Talk about these questions in a small group.

1. For what purpose does the writer mention shoe sizes in paragraph 1? What is the main idea of this paragraph? According to the writer, what is "the usual sleep schedule?" Is this *your* usual sleep schedule? If it is not, explain.

2. The reading says, "A sleep cycle takes you from light sleep to deep sleep and back again. It includes the four stages of NREM sleep and then a short period of REM sleep" (paragraph 4). According to this basic definition, all sleep cycles are the same. How does the line graph show more detailed information about a series of sleep cycles? Does the graph show an average night's sleep, as defined in paragraph 1 of the reading? Explain.

3. What effects of not getting enough sleep does the writer mention in paragraph 8? What other effects can you add to the list? Have you experienced these other effects, or are they effects that you see, or hear about, in other people? Explain your answer.

4. Why does the writer suggest that you "think about sleep stages if you set an alarm?" What other advice does the writer give and why? Do you think you will follow any of the writer's advice? Tell why or why not.

Interview

Work with a partner, and take turns asking the questions below.* Write your partner's answers. Use numbers:

| 0 = No | 1 = Probably not | 2 = Maybe | 3 = Probably |

Would you fall asleep while you were...

1. sitting and reading? ____

2. watching TV? ____

3. riding in a car for an hour? ____

4. lying down in the afternoon? ____

5. sitting and talking to someone? ____

6. sitting quietly after lunch? ____

7. sitting in a car that is stopped in traffic for a few minutes? ____

   Your partner's total: ☐

Add up the numbers, and tell your partner the total.

   0–6: That's great! You're getting enough sleep.

   7–8: You're average.

   9 and up: Get more sleep!

* Based on the Epworth Sleepiness Scale designed by Murray W. Johns, M.D.

WRITING

A. Use the Target Vocabulary: Choose five target words or phrases from the list on page 166. On a piece of paper, use each word or phrase in a sentence. Underline the target vocabulary. Then find a partner and read each other's sentences.

B. Practice Writing: Choose one of these topics and write a paragraph about it. Then find a partner and read each other's paragraphs.

1. Do you get enough sleep in general? What happens when you don't get enough?

2. Think of someone you know who does not get enough sleep. Imagine you are writing them a letter or an email. Explain what you know about sleep and how too little sleep affects people.

CHAPTER 16

In Your Dreams

Beatle Paul McCartney dreamed up "Yesterday."

GETTING READY TO READ

Talk about these questions in a small group.

1. What do you remember about your dreams?

2. Have you ever gotten a good idea while you were sleeping? If not, do you think it seems possible? Explain.

3. Did you know that animals dream? What do you think they dream about?

READING

Read to Find Out: What questions about dreams are researchers trying to answer?

Look at the pictures, words, and definitions next to the reading. Then read without stopping.

In Your Dreams

1   Bruno Beckham has a good job. He also has a new job offer. He has to make a decision **right away**, but he's not sure **whether** he should accept the offer. He *is* sure, however, that he's not going to **make up his mind** tonight. "I'll know what to do in the morning," he says. How will he know? What does he think will happen overnight?[1] "I don't know," he says, "but **whenever** I have a big decision to make, I have to sleep on it."

[1] *overnight =
continuing all
night*

2   When you face a big decision, do your friends tell you to sleep on it? People in Italy say, "Dormici su." It means the same thing. In France, they say, "La nuit porte conseil," meaning "The night brings advice." People in many cultures believe that something **useful** happens during sleep, but what happens, and why?

[2] *a boxer*

3   Maybe the answer can be found in our dreams. Many people believe that dreams help us in our **daily** lives. The American boxer[2] Floyd Patterson believed this. He used to dream of new ways to move in a fight, and he **claimed** that these moves helped him surprise other boxers. Srinivasa Ramanujan, an important mathematician[3] from India, said that all his **discoveries** came to him in dreams. Artists, scientists, and writers report getting ideas from dreams, too. The English writer Mary Shelley did. She said that the story of Frankenstein came to her in a dream. Paul McCartney of the Beatles woke up one morning from a dream in which he was listening to music. He immediately went to the piano and played the music, which became "Yesterday," one of the Beatles' most famous songs.

[3] *mathematician
= someone
who does
research in
math*

4   Scientists do not agree on what dreams mean or why people dream. Some doubt that dreams have any important purpose. They say that dreams show activity in the brain, but it's like the activity of a car going in circles with no driver. It does nothing useful. **On the other hand**, many scientists claim that dreams are helpful. They say that dreams are good for learning new skills and developing strong memories.

Mary Shelley's monster

5   Some researchers hope to learn more about the dreams of people by studying the dreams of animals. At the Massachusetts Institute of Technology (MIT), scientists have studied the dreams of rats. In one study, the rats were learning to run through a maze,[4] and the scientists would **record** the activity in the rats' brains. Later, during REM sleep, the rats' brains showed exactly the same activity. The rats were going through the maze again in their dreams. Researchers could tell if the dreaming rats were running or standing **still**. **In fact**, one researcher reported that they could pinpoint[5] where the rats would be in the maze if they were awake.

[4] *a rat in a maze*

6   Were the rats practicing for the next day? Does dreaming **somehow** help them learn and remember? Do human brains work this way? The researchers at MIT **are searching** for answers to these questions. Right now, there is no **explanation** for dreams that everyone accepts. There is a great deal we still do not know about the sleeping brain, but maybe one day we will know all its secrets.

[5] *pinpoint =* show exactly where something is

Quick Comprehension Check

A. Read these sentences **about the reading**. Circle T (true) or F (false). On the line, write the number of the paragraph with the answer.

1.   Only human beings dream.   T   F   _____

2.   Bruno Beckham says sleep helps him make decisions.   T   F   _____

3.   According to some famous people, good ideas come in dreams.   T   F   _____

4.   Scientists all agree: There is one basic reason why we dream.   T   F   _____

5.   Scientists have the technology to study brain activity during dreams.   T   F   _____

6.   Dreams may help us learn and remember.   T   F   _____

B. Work with your class. Share your answers from part A. Go back to the reading to find the reason why a statement is true or false. Correct the false statements.

EXPLORING VOCABULARY

Thinking about the Target Vocabulary

A. Look at the chart with the target vocabulary. Two nouns, three verbs, and two adjectives are missing. Scan the reading to find them. Add them to the correct places in the chart. Write the singular form of any plural noun. Write the base form of each verb.

¶	Nouns	Verbs	Adjectives	Other
1				right away
				whether
				make up (your) mind
				whenever
2				
3				
4				on the other hand
5				
				still
				in fact
6				somehow

B. Which target words or phrases are new to you? Circle them in the chart. Then find them in the reading. Look at the context. Can you guess the meaning?

Using the Target Vocabulary

A. These sentences are **about the reading**. Complete them with the words and phrases in the box.

claimed	in fact	searching	still	whenever
explanation	on the other hand	somehow	useful	whether

1. Bruno isn't sure if he wants to accept his new job offer. He doesn't know

   _____ to accept it or not.

2. Every time that he faces a big decision, Bruno sleeps on it. This means,

   _____ Bruno has a big decision to make, he waits until

   morning to decide.

3. Many people believe that while we sleep, something

   _____ happens, something that helps us.

4. The boxer Floyd Patterson said that his dreams helped him win

   fights. Was it true? No one knows for sure. However, that is what he

   _____.

5. Some scientists say that dreams have no effect on us. _____,

   many others say that dreams help us learn and remember.

6. Sometimes the rats moved through the maze. At other times, they

   did not move. They stood _____.

7. The scientists could tell if the sleeping rats were running through the

   maze in their dreams. _____, they could do even more:

   They could tell exactly where in the maze a rat was.

8. Was dreaming useful to the rats in some way? Did it

   _____ help them?

9. The researchers at MIT are looking for answers to the question "Why

   do we dream?" They are _____ for answers.

10. So far, no one has explained dreams in a way that everyone accepts. We

   have no good _____ for them.

B. These sentences use the target words and phrases **in new contexts**.
Complete them with the words and phrases in the box.

claimed	in fact	searching	still	whenever
explanation	on the other hand	somehow	useful	whether

1. I don't know how he did it, but _____, he managed to win.

2. Stop moving! You must keep _____ when I take

   your picture.

3. Gloria couldn't decide _____ to cut her hair or let it keep growing.

4. The police are _____ for the missing child.

5. The president of the company believes in naps. _____, he takes one almost every day.

Vocabulary Tip: *Search for something* means to try hard to find it. *Search +* a place means to look all through that place: *The police searched the house. Search* can also be a noun: *I did an online search for the closest drugstore.*

6. I heard that song yesterday and thought of you. In fact, I think of you _____ I hear that song .

7. I don't understand why Helen was so angry. Did she give you any _____?

8. You want to store _____ facts in long-term memory and remember them later.

9. Bob _____ that his dog could read his mind, but I think Bob was imagining things.

10. Chris has two job offers. The first one pays better; _____, the second one sounds more secure. A secure job or a better-paying one—which should he choose?

C. Read each definition and look at the paragraph number. Look back at the reading on pages 175–176 to find the **boldfaced** word or phrase to match the definition. Copy it in the chart.

Definition	Paragraph	Target Word or Phrase
1. very soon, immediately	1	
2. decide	1	
3. happening every day	3	
4. new facts, or answers to a question, that someone learns	3	
5. store sounds or pictures on something so they can be listened to or seen again	5	

Building on the Vocabulary

Studying Collocations: Phrases with *Right*

Several phrases with *right* + adverb mean "immediately" or "very soon." Look at these examples of phrases with *right*:

- *I need the money right away.*
- *I'm coming right back. / I'll be right back.*
- *We're leaving right now.*

Write three sentences using the three phrases above with *right*.

1. _____

2. _____

3. _____

DEVELOPING YOUR READING SKILLS

Scanning

Read these statements about "In Your Dreams." Scan the reading for the information you need to complete them. Answers inside quotation marks (" ") must match the words in the reading exactly.

1. If you think someone should wait a day before making a decision, you can

   suggest that they " _____."

2. Some famous people have said that dreams _____.

3. Scientists disagree about what _____ and why

   _____.

4. Some scientists claim that "dreams are good for _____."

5. Some scientists are studying the dreams of animals because

   _____.

6. In one study on rats at MIT, the rats were learning how to find their way

   through a _____. In their sleep, they

   _____.

Fact vs. Opinion

A. Decide if each statement is a fact or an opinion. Base your answers on information from the reading. Circle *Fact* or *Opinion*.

1. There is activity in the brain while we sleep.   Fact / Opinion

2. Our dreams send us important messages.   Fact / Opinion

3. Some famous people have believed in the power of dreams.   Fact / Opinion

4. Dreams have no meaning.   Fact / Opinion

5. MIT scientists have studied the dreams of rats.   Fact / Opinion

6. In the future, scientists will discover why we dream.   Fact / Opinion

> **Vocabulary Tip:**
> *Vs.* (or *v*) is the abbreviation of *versus*, meaning "as opposed to or against." It is used for two things being contrasted, two teams in a sports event, or two sides in a court case.

B. Write two sentences.

1. Write a fact about dreams from "In Your Dreams."

_____

_____

2. Write an opinion of your own about dreams.

_____

_____

Summarizing

Write answers to these seven questions on a piece of paper. Then use your answers to write a summary of the reading. Write your summary as a paragraph.

1. When do people say "sleep on it"?

2. Why do they say it?

3. What do some people say dreams can do?

4. What example can you give of dreams being useful to someone?

5. What do scientists say about the meaning and purpose of dreams?

6. Why do scientists study the dreams of animals?

7. What is one possible reason for dreaming?

One student began her summary like this:

> People often say "Sleep on it!" to someone who needs to make a big decision. They think something helpful happens in our brains while we sleep and dream.

CRITICAL THINKING

Discussion

Talk about these questions in a small group.

1. What does Bruno Beckham believe about making important decisions? Do you agree with him? Tell why or why not. Is there an expression in your first language that has the same meaning as "sleep on it"?

2. The first sentence of paragraph 3 mentions "the answer." What is the question? What is the main idea of this paragraph? What support for this idea does the writer give? How are the people mentioned in the paragraph alike, and how are they different?

3. What two groups of scientists are described in paragraph 4? What would scientists from each group say to Bruno Beckham? Which group do you think is more interesting to the writer of this text? Explain your answer with examples from the reading.

4. What research is discussed in the reading? What did the researchers learn from it? If the same thing is true for both sleeping rats and sleeping human beings, what might that mean for a student?

> **Critical Thinking Tip:** An important critical thinking skill is being able to take information you read and apply it to another situation.

5. Many studies have been done on people who were dreaming. Would you volunteer to take part in research like that, or would you like to do that kind of research? Explain your answer.

WRITING

A. Use the Target Vocabulary: Choose five target words or phrases from the list on page 177. On a piece of paper, use each word or phrase in a sentence. Underline the target vocabulary. Then find a partner and read each other's sentences.

B. Practice Writing: Choose one of these topics and write a paragraph about it. Then find a partner and read each other's paragraphs.

1. Whenever Bruno Beckham faces a big decision, he sleeps on it. What do you do? What, or who, helps you make decisions?

2. Think about a time when you had to make a choice. What did you decide? How did you make your decision? Do you think it was the right one? Why or why not?

> **Writing Tip:** Before you start writing a paragraph, it helps to get some ideas down on paper quickly. Just make notes, or try drawing a concept map (or idea web) as on page 103.

Checkpoint

LEARNING OUTCOME

❯ Review and expand on the content of Unit 4

LOOK BACK

A. Think About This

Look back at your answers to the *Think About This* question on page 143:
How much do you know about your brain?
Do you want to change any of your answers?

B. Remember the Readings

What do you want to remember most from the readings in Unit 4? For each chapter, write one sentence about the reading.

Chapter 13: Food for Thought

_____

Chapter 14: Your Memory at Work

_____

Chapter 15: Sleep and the Brain

_____

Chapter 16: In Your Dreams

_____

REVIEWING VOCABULARY

A. Complete the sentences with words and phrases from the box. There are two extra words or phrases.

according to	on the other hand	search	that is
get over	or so	somehow	whenever
no matter	right away	store	whether

1. I don't know _____ I'll go or stay. I have to make up my mind.

2. He wants it so much that he says he has to have it, _____ the price!

3. _____ the weather report, the rain should end soon.

4. Come _____ you want. I'll be home all day.

5. I don't remember how long the lecture was—an hour _____, I think.

6. Call if you need me, and I'll come _____.

7. These shoes are much more expensive than those, but _____, they're more comfortable and better looking. So maybe they are worth the extra cost.

8. He didn't have a ticket to the show, so I don't know how he got in to see it. He must've talked his way in _____.

9. It took me two weeks to _____ my cold.

10. We will _____ the Internet for the information we need.

B. Complete the sentences with words from the box. There are two extra words.

claimed	discovery	imagined	meant	realize	series
concerns	divided	include	periods	review	term

1. He had a lot of homework. That _____ that he couldn't go out.

2. Her research _____ the connections between sleep and memory.

3. This building is _____ into ten apartments.

4. Does the rent for the apartment _____ heat and electricity, or is that extra?

5. Reporters had many questions about the scientist's latest _____.

6. After a long _____ of meetings, they came to an agreement.

7. One driver _____ that the other driver was going too fast.

8. In his dream, he _____ that he was flying.

9. We expect a cloudy day with some _____ of rain during the afternoon.

10. Unfortunately, he didn't _____ how long it would take to get there, so he was late.

EXPANDING VOCABULARY

Choose the correct member from each word family to complete sentences 1–8 below.

	Nouns	Verbs	Adjectives	Adverbs
1.	activity		active	actively
2.	creation	create	creative	creatively
3.	effect		effective	effectively
4.	increase	increase	increasing	increasingly
5.	influence	influence	influential	
6.	luck		lucky	luckily
7.	use	use	useful	usefully
8.	weakness	weaken	weak	weakly

1. The brain is _____ during REM sleep.

2. The government reported the _____ of 50,000 new jobs.

3. His family troubles are having an _____ on his work.

4. _____ numbers of people are questioning the president's decision.

5. Please talk to him. Maybe you can use your _____ to get him to change his mind.

6. _____, she managed to get to the station in time for her train.

7. He bought a new computer and now has no _____ for his old one.

8. Powerful storms over the ocean usually _____ as they pass over land.

A PUZZLE

There are 12 target words from Unit 4 in this puzzle. The words go across (→) and down (↓). Find the words and circle them. Then use them to complete the sentences below.

```
X  I  Q  V  X  N  A  P  M  X  D  E
K  M  H  M  R  E  G  I  O  N  V  X
L  M  W  P  D  X  P  W  Q  V  X  P
F  E  E  D  G  Z  R  S  T  I  L  L
W  D  S  E  A  S  O  N  F  W  H  A
Z  I  J  V  X  P  N  V  O  Z  K  N
D  A  I  L  Y  K  O  X  C  J  X  A
X  T  V  X  G  Q  U  P  U  X  T  T
W  E  I  G  H  T  N  Z  S  K  W  I
T  L  X  Z  K  W  C  J  X  W  Z  O
H  Y  C  O  N  N  E  C  T  I  O  N
```

ACROSS

1. Do they see the _____ between human activity and changes in the weather?

2. We _____ our cat twice a day.

3. Please stand _____ while I take your picture.

4. He's trying to lose _____ by eating less and walking more.

5. His _____ schedule is very full.

6. That _____ of France is famous for cheese.

7. The baby is tired and needs her _____.

8. Plants grow quickly during the rainy _____.

DOWN

1. The boss will expect an _____ when you're late for work.

2. How do you _____ your last name?

3. They called 911 and explained the emergency. The police came

_____.

4. Pay attention, children! You need to _____ on getting your homework done.

BUILDING DICTIONARY SKILLS

A. Look at the entry for the verb *set*. Write the number of the meaning used in each sentence below.

_____ **a.** His parents want him to **set** an example for his little brother.

_____ **b.** **Set** the timer for five minutes.

_____ **c.** Have they **set** a date for their wedding?

_____ **d.** Please **set** the boxes on that table.

> **Vocabulary Tip:** Many words have more than one meaning. When you look up a word in the dictionary, you may need to read through several meanings to find the one you need.

---

set¹ /sɛt/ *v* past tense and past participle **set**, present participle **setting**
1 ▸ PUT STH SOMEWHERE ◂ [T] to carefully put something down somewhere: *Just **set** that bag **down** on the floor.* | *He took off his watch and **set it on** the dresser.*
2 ▸ STANDARD ◂ [T] to decide something that other things are compared to or measured against: *The agency has **set standards** for water cleanliness.* | *Parents should **set an example** for their children* (=behave in the way they want their children to behave).

3 ▸ PRICE/TIME ETC. ◂ [T] to decide that something will happen at a particular time, cost a particular amount, etc.: *The judge plans to **set a date** for the trial.* | *Officials have not yet **set a price** on how much the study will cost.*
4 ▸ CLOCK/MACHINE ◂ [T] to move part of a clock or a piece of equipment so that it will do what you want it to do: *I **set my alarm** for 6:30.*
5 ▸ START STH HAPPENING ◂ [I,T] to make something start happening or to make someone start doing something: *Angry mobs **set** the building **on** fire.*

B. Look at this entry for the verb *apply*. Write the number of the meaning used in each sentence below.

_____ **a.** The new rule **applies** to all students.

_____ **b.** We **applied** two coats of paint.

_____ **c.** He is **applying** for several jobs.

---

ap•ply /əˈplaɪ/ *v* (**applied**, **applies**) **1** [I] to make a formal, especially written, request for a job, place at a college, permission to do something, etc.: *Fifteen people **applied for** the job.* | *He has **applied for** U.S. citizenship.* | *Anna **applied to** several colleges in California.* **2** [I,T] to have an effect on, involve or concern a particular person, group, or situation: *The nutrition labeling requirements **apply to** most foods.* **3** [T] to use a method, idea, etc. in a particular situation, activity, or process: *Internships give students a chance to **apply** their skills in real situations.* **4** [T] to put something on a surface or press on the surface of something: ***Apply** the lotion evenly.*

Vocabulary Self-Test 2

Circle the letter of the word or phrase that best completes each sentence.

1. They never keep large _____ of money in the store.

   a. waves   b. amounts   c. activities   d. connections

2. Neighbors offered to help Tina _____ for her lost cat.

   a. pronounce   b. look up   c. search   d. include

3. I don't know _____ how much it costs, but I know it's expensive.

   a. exactly   b. immediately   c. whenever   d. while

4. He believes in "Murphy's law." _____, he believes that if anything can go wrong, it will.

   a. Luckily   b. Or so   c. In the first place   d. That is

5. The fire _____ the building, but no one was hurt.

   a. destroyed   b. created   c. attracted   d. developed

6. He needs more time to _____ his mind.

   a. make sure   b. pay attention   c. make sense   d. make up

7. After all their _____ to find a better apartment, they decided to stay where they are.

   a. explanations   b. efforts   c. surfaces   d. periods

8. People from TV and radio were at the White House to _____ the U.S. president's every word.

   a. divide   b. imagine   c. record   d. feed

9. Arunaa got tired of the man staring at her and decided that she wouldn't _____ it any longer.

   a. store   b. recycle   c. go on   d. put up with

10. Boyan is working on the problem of ocean pollution and hoping to

    _____.

    a. make a   b. connect   c. get over   d. have something in
       difference   common

11. Several workers were out sick, creating a difficult _____ for
    the other people in the office.

    a. memory   b. nature   c. interest   d. situation

12. Not everyone will be invited, only _____ people.

    a. alive   b. certain   c. daily   d. entire

13. You did half the work, so it wouldn't be _____ for you to get
    less than half the money.

    a. relaxed   b. active   c. fair   d. useful

14. Her father made her turn off the TV and _____ on her
    homework.

    a. focus   b. float   c. apply   d. claim

15. Your heart _____ goes up when you run.

    a. pollution   b. dirt   c. rate   d. increase

16. Nothing seems to help, _____ what I try.

    a. no matter   b. on the   c. in fact   d. in all
                       other hand

17. When I travel and enter a new time zone, I always _____ my
    watch to local time.

    a. set   b. concern   c. affect   d. draw

18. It was terrible news, and we found it difficult to control our

    _____.

    a. seasons   b. emotions   c. storms   d. discoveries

19. Please stay _____ but get out of the building as fast as you can.

    a. national   b. calm   c. weak   d. advanced

20. The area known as the Farm Belt _____ most of the nation's
    meat and grains.

    a. supplies   b. complains   c. reviews   d. realizes

21. The point of the law is to fight pollution and protect the _____.

    a. system   b. heat   c. environment   d. weight

22. The cerebral cortex is a _____ of the brain that plays a key role in memory.

   a. technology   b. region   c. shell   d. mess

23. The doctor's quiet voice and _____ touch made his young patients trust him.

   a. violent   b. powerful   c. gentle   d. sharp

24. Is there room to put these coats and hats in your _____?

   a. planet   b. coast   c. closet   d. nap

25. They are showing a _____ of films, starting at 4:00 P.M. and ending after midnight.

   a. series   b. volunteer   c. space   d. base

26. All this ice and snow on the roads will no doubt _____ more road accidents.

   a. contain   b. mean   c. attach   d. schedule

27. _____ the newspapers, no one was seriously hurt.

   a. Somehow   b. According to c. Basically   d. Still

28. This plane can hold _____ 120 people, while that one has space for only 80.

   a. right away   b. off   c. whether   d. up to

29. After class, the students reviewed their _____ to prepare for the test.

   a. lecture   b. term   c. notes   d. influence

See the Answer Key on page 239.

COMMUNICATION

THINK ABOUT THIS

What do people do to communicate? Add to the lists.

Things people do

speak

Tools people use

pens

Who Does It Better?

Elephants in conversation?

GETTING READY TO READ

Do this task in a small group.

Look at the chart. Which types of communication do human beings use? Which types do animals use? Check ☑ your answers. Give at least one example for each checked answer.

	Words	Sounds	Movement	Smells
Humans	☑ *hello*	☐	☐	☐
Animals	☐	☐	☐	☐

READING

Read to Find Out: What examples of animal communication are found in the reading?

Look at the pictures, words, and definitions next to the reading. Then read without stopping.

Who Does It Better?

1   Who is better at communicating, people or animals? If you think about human **inventions**, such as the telephone and the Internet, the answer seems perfectly clear. Human beings are "The Great Communicators." However, think about your own **personal** communication skills. If you compare your skills with what animals can do, the answer is not so simple. Animals can communicate in ways that people cannot.

[1] an opera singer

2   Most of us depend on our **voices** for much of our communication. We use words and sounds to pass information to the people around us. However, the sound of the human voice cannot travel very far. Even the voice of an opera singer[1] with years of **training** cannot travel as far as many animal voices. Think of the elephant, for example. Because of its great size, its voice has the power to be heard for miles. Elephants can also make very **low** sounds, too deep for any human to hear, which let them communicate over even greater **distances**. These sounds travel in sound waves[2] both through the air and through **the ground**. How do elephants receive the messages? No one knows. Maybe they hear them with their ears, or maybe they **sense** them in some other way. It's possible that the sound waves pass from the ground through the elephants' toenails[3] into their bones and then to their brains!

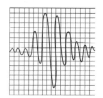

[2] a way to picture sound waves

3   Let's also consider communication **through** movement. Professional dancers use dance to share ideas and emotions. When we watch them, we may be able to understand what they are saying with their bodies. But even a great dancer's ability to speak through movement cannot match the average honeybee's. Bees do a dance that tells other bees where to find food. The dance tells the other bees which way to go so they can fly to the food in a **straight** line. It also tells them exactly how far to go. It clearly describes both the **direction** and the distance to a specific place.

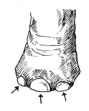

[3] an elephant's toenails

A honeybee

4   The sense of smell offers another way to communicate. People can get information through their sense of smell, as when your nose tells you something good is cooking in the kitchen. In general, however, we don't use smells to send messages the way that animals do. For example, certain animals produce smells to tell others "This is my

place—get out!" A smell can also give an **invitation**. Often a **female** animal will produce a smell to attract a **male**. It tells him, "Here I am—come find me." Animals are also better than humans at understanding the messages in smells. We certainly cannot **compete** with dogs. The canine sense of smell is up to one million times better than ours.

5   Our noses are not the best, our voices are not the strongest, and our dancing may not say anything at all. But people are the only ones with words and written languages. So maybe we can still call ourselves "The Great Communicators."

Quick Comprehension Check

A. Read these sentences. Circle T (true) or F (false). On the line, write the number of the paragraph with the answer.

1. Humans communicate better than animals in every way.   T   F   _____
2. Elephants can make sounds that travel very far.   T   F   _____
3. Bees can communicate with other bees through movement.   T   F   _____
4. A male honeybee dances to attract a female.   T   F   _____
5. Both animals and people use their noses to get information.   T   F   _____
6. People use both sound and movement to communicate.   T   F   _____

B. Work with your class. Share your answers from part A. Go back to the reading to find the reason why a statement is true or false. Correct the false statements.

EXPLORING VOCABULARY

Thinking about the Target Vocabulary

A. Look at the chart with the target vocabulary. Eight nouns and two verbs are missing. Scan the reading to find them, and add them to the correct places in the chart. Write the singular form of any plural noun. Write the base form of the verb.

¶	Nouns	Verbs	Adjectives	Other
1				
			personal	

¶	Nouns	Verbs	Adjectives	Other
2				
			low	
3				through
			straight	
4				
			female	

B. Which target words or phrases are new to you? Circle them in the chart. Then find them in the reading. Look at the context. Can you guess the meaning?

Using the Target Vocabulary

A. These sentences are **about the reading**. Complete them with the words in the box.

compete	inventions	low	personal	through
direction	invitation	male	sense	voice

1. People have invented many tools to help them communicate. Two

   examples of such _____ are the telephone and the Internet.

2. Each person has his or her own _____ communication

   skills. These are the skills that belong to that one person.

3. When you speak or sing, you use your _____. Other people

   hear it.

4. Elephants can make, and hear, sounds that are too _____ for the human ear. We cannot hear them because they are not high enough.

5. Elephants hear with their ears. They may also _____ very low sounds through their toenails and their bones. It is not clear exactly how they become aware of these sounds.

Vocabulary Tip: Use *sense* when someone becomes aware of something without knowing exactly how they become aware of it: *He said nothing, but I sensed that something was wrong.*

6. Some animals, like bees, communicate _____ movement. They use movement to send messages.

7. The bee's dance tells other bees which way to go. It tells them the _____ to fly in to find food.

8. A female animal may produce a smell to get the attention of a _____ animal. She uses smell to communicate with him.

9. When a female animal produces a smell to invite a male to come and find her, we can say she is sending him an _____.

Vocabulary Tip: *Compete* (*with* or *against* someone) means "try to win." However, if you *cannot* compete with someone, it means they are far better than you are.

10. The canine sense of smell is much, much better than the human sense of smell. In other words, our sense of smell cannot _____ with the dog's.

B. These sentences use the target words **in new contexts**. Complete them with the words in the box.

compete	inventions	low	personal	through
direction	invitation	male	senses	voices

1. Yoko phoned me with an _____ to a party. I thanked her and said I would be happy to go.

2. The scientist made his discoveries _____ years of hard work.

Vocabulary Tip: *Through* often means from one end to another of a place or a thing (*I walked through the store*), but *through* can also mean "by using or doing or by means of."

3. The wheel is one of the most important _____ in human history.

4. The driver turned the car around and drove away in the opposite _____.

5. If an animal _____ danger, it may communicate to other animals that they need to hide or escape.

6. Men who sing usually have deeper _____ than women singers do.

7. He has learned about the business world both in school and through his own _____ experience.

Vocabulary Tip:
The words *male* and *female* can be nouns or adjectives. Use them as nouns only when speaking of animals, not people.

8. Teams from many countries _____ against each other at the Olympic games.

9. _____ elephants are generally larger than females.

10. A piano makes _____ sounds when you play the keys on the left end of the keyboard. The higher notes are to the right.

C. Read the sentences. Guess the meaning of the **boldfaced** target words and phrases from the context. Match them with their definitions.

  a. Make sure you plant the tree a safe **distance** from the house.

  b. *Waitress* is a word sometimes used for a **female** server in a restaurant.

  c. Leaves fell from the trees and covered **the ground**.

  d. We placed the chairs in a **straight** line.

  e. It takes years of education and **training** to become a doctor.

Target Word or Phrase	**Definition**
1. _____	= the surface of the earth; what you walk on outdoors
2. _____	= going in one direction only, not bending or curving
3. _____	= the amount of space between two places or things
4. _____	= belonging to the sex that can have babies or produce eggs
5. _____	= the process of learning the skills for a certain job or activity

Building on the Vocabulary

> ### Word Grammar: Meanings and Uses of *Low*
>
> The word *low* is usually an adjective. It can describe
>
> - a quiet or deep sound: *a low whisper, a low voice*
> - something that isn't high or tall: *a low wall, a low building*
> - a small amount or number: *low-fat food, low grades*
> - the bad nature of something: *a low opinion, a low trick*
>
> *Low* can also be
>
> - an adverb *(The plane was flying low.)*
> - a noun *(Prices fell to a new low.)*

Is **low** a noun (n.), an adjective (adj.), or an adverb (adv.) in each sentence? Circle your answers.

1. The TV sits on a low table.   n.   adj.   adv.
2. Everybody's life has its highs and lows.   n.   adj.   adv.
3. Shoppers like low prices.   n.   adj.   adv.
4. He threw the ball low.   n.   adj.   adv.
5. I got a low score on the test.   n.   adj.   adv.

DEVELOPING YOUR READING SKILLS

Reading for Details

Are these statements about the reading true or false? If the reading doesn't give the information, check (✓) *It doesn't say.*

	True	False	It doesn't say.
1. We depend on our voices for much of our communication with other people.			
2. Elephants have the best hearing of any animals.			
3. Sound waves can travel only through the air.			
4. The dance of the honeybee tells other bees which way to go to find food.			
5. The dance of the honeybee tells other bees what kind of food they will find.			

	True	False	It doesn't say.
6. All living things use smells to communicate.			
7. Most of a dog's brain is used for reading (or understanding) smells.			
8. Words give human beings a very special way to communicate.			

Using Graphic Organizers

Complete this diagram of the reading. Write the topics of paragraphs 2, 3, and 4. You do not need to write complete sentences.

Who Does It Better?		
1. (Introduction) People vs. animals—comparing communication skills		
	2.	
	3.	
	4.	
5. (Conclusion) People win—we have words, written language		

Reading Tip: The last words of a reading can be important. Sometimes they show the writer's purpose or the point of the reading.

Main Ideas and Supporting Details

A. Match the main ideas and the details that support them. Write the letters.

Main Ideas	Supporting Details
____ 1. Certain inventions help people communicate.	a. Bees do a dance to tell other bees where food is.
____ 2. The human voice can't travel as far as some animal voices.	b. A female animal may produce a smell to attract a male.
____ 3. Some animals communicate through movement.	c. Think of the telephone and the Internet.
____ 4. Animals sometimes use smells to communicate with other animals.	d. Think of the canine sense of smell, for example.
____ 5. People can't compete with animals in some ways.	e. An elephant's voice can be heard for miles.

B. Think of another example to support each of the Main Ideas in exercise A. Write complete sentences.

1. <u>Inventions like pens and paper let people write to each other.</u>

2. _____

3. _____

4. _____

5. _____

CRITICAL THINKING

Discussion

Talk about these questions in a small group.

1. According to the writer, who is better at communicating, people or animals? Underline the sentence in paragraph 5 that gives the basis for the writer's conclusion. Do you agree? If you do, add other evidence to support that conclusion. If you disagree, give evidence to support your opinion.

2. The reading says that animals can communicate in ways we cannot. Find examples in the reading. What other examples can you give of animals that communicate in amazing ways?

3. The reading says that dance is a form of human communication. Do you agree? Explain your answer. What does the writer mean by "our dancing may not say anything at all"? In what other ways do people use movement to communicate?

4. According to the reading, people don't usually communicate through smell. But what are people saying when they put on perfume, cologne, or aftershave? Is this a form of communication? Explain your answer.

> **Critical Thinking Tip:** When a writer reaches a **conclusion**, it means they come to a decision after considering all the information (or evidence) they have. You may or may not come to the same conclusion as the writer.

WRITING

A. Use the Target Vocabulary: Choose five target words or phrases from the list on pages 194–195. On a piece of paper, use each word or phrase in a sentence. Underline the target vocabulary. Then find a partner and read each other's sentences.

B. Practice Writing: Choose one of these topics and write a paragraph about it. Then find a partner and read each other's paragraphs.

1. Pets sometimes play an important part in people's lives. People communicate with their pets in several ways. Have you ever had a pet? How do or did you communicate?

2. What kind of animal would you like to be? Why? Tell both the good and the bad things about being this kind of animal.

> **Writing Tip:** Consider adding a photo of the animal you are writing about, especially if it is a kind of animal your reader may not know much about.

CHAPTER 18

When and Why We Laugh

"The oil in the social machine"

GETTING READY TO READ

Talk about these questions in a small group.

1. Ask one person in your group to make himself or herself laugh. Then talk about what happened in your group when this person laughed, or tried to.

2. Would it surprise you to learn that some kinds of animals laugh? What kinds of animals do you think can laugh? What do you think makes them laugh?

Read to Find Out: Why do people laugh?

Look at the words and definitions next to the reading. Then read without stopping.

When and Why We Laugh

1 People have many ways to **express** themselves—that is, to show how they feel or what they think. One way that feels especially good is **laughter**. We all laugh when we see or hear something funny. We also laugh when we see other people laughing, which is why we say laughter is contagious.[1] Laughter clearly has a role to play in human communication, but what are we saying when we laugh?

2 A team of psychologists[2] studied the laughter of 120 students at a U.S. university by having the students watch funny movies. Sometimes the students were alone, and sometimes they were in pairs. The psychologists recorded the students' laughter, and they noticed that the students made a wide variety of laughing sounds. They also noticed differences in how many times each student laughed and how the student laughed. For the students in pairs, both these things depended on the student's partner: Was the other person the same sex or the opposite sex? And what was the relationship between the two—was the person a friend or a **stranger**? Here are some of the researchers' findings:[3]

- Men laughed much more during the movies when they were with a friend. It did not matter whether the friend was male or female. Men laughed much less when their partner was a stranger or when they were alone.

- Women laughed most when they were with male friends. With male strangers, women laughed in a higher voice.

- There were three basic types of laughs: high songlike laughs, laughs with the sounds coming mostly through the nose, and low grunting[4] laughs.

3 The researchers then **carried out** another **study**, in which they asked people to listen to these three types of laughter. To find out which kind of laughter people liked best, they asked questions like: Does the person laughing sound friendly? Do you think he or she sounds **attractive**? Would you like to meet this person? Most people **preferred** the high songlike sounds and were attracted to people who laughed this way.

4 The researchers believe that laughter is a tool we use, usually without thinking about it, to influence the emotions and **behavior** of other people. They say we often use laughter to show that we want to

[1] *contagious* = easily passed from one person to another, like a cold

[2] *psychologist* = someone trained in the study of the mind and how it works

[3] *findings* = the information someone learns as a result of research

[4] *grunting* = short, low sounds people make in their throats

be friends. In fact, **in spite of** what you may think, most laughter during conversation is *not* because someone is reacting to[5] something funny. Researcher Robert Provine, author of *Laughter: A Scientific Investigation*, says that in conversation, the people who are listening **actually** laugh less than the ones who are speaking. A speaker's laughter has a **social** purpose, says Provine. He calls laughter "the oil in the social machine." **In other words**, it helps relationships between people work **smoothly**.

5   Did you know that human beings are not the only ones who laugh? Dogs do it, too. Canine laughter sounds something like "Huh, huh, huh," and it seems to express the idea "Let's play!" Another researcher, Jaak Panksepp, reports that rats laugh, too. The white rats he works with in his **lab** laugh when he tickles[6] them. But please do not go out and try this. Panksepp **warns**, "You have to know the rat."

[5] *reacting to =* acting or feeling a certain way because of something that happened

[6] *tickle =* touch someone to make them laugh

Quick Comprehension Check

A. Read these sentences. Circle T (true) or F (false). On the line, write the number of the paragraph with the answer.

1. Laughter is part of human communication.   T   F   _____

2. Only human beings laugh.   T   F   _____

3. The people we are with affect how we laugh.   T   F   _____

4. The college students in the study laughed   T   F   _____
    only with their friends.

5. Researchers say that we laugh to influence   T   F   _____
    other people.

6. People in conversation usually laugh because   T   F   _____
    they hear something funny.

B. Work with your class. Share your answers from part A. Go back to the reading to find the reason why a statement is true or false. Correct the false statements.

EXPLORING VOCABULARY

Thinking about the Target Vocabulary

A. Look at the chart with the target vocabulary. Five nouns, four verbs, and two adjectives are missing. Scan the reading to find them, and add them to the correct places in the chart. Write the singular form of any plural noun. Write the base form of each verb.

¶	Nouns	Verbs	Adjectives	Other
1				
2				
3				
4				
				in spite of
				actually
				in other words
				smoothly
5				

B. Which target words or phrases are new to you? Circle them in the chart. Then find them in the reading. Look at the context. Can you guess the meaning?

Using the Target Vocabulary

A. These sentences are **about the reading**. Complete them with the words and phrases in the box.

actually	express	in spite of	laughter	social
behavior	in other words	lab	preferred	warned

1. People communicate their ideas and emotions with words. We can also _____ ourselves with sounds—by laughing, for example.

2. When we laugh, it sometimes makes other people laugh, too, so we say that _____ is contagious.

3. Researchers asked people to listen to three types of laughter and choose the one they liked best. Most people _____ the same type.

4. Researchers say we use laughter to influence what other people do. That is, we use it to influence the _____ of other people.

5. It's natural to think that when people laugh in conversation, it's because they heard something funny. But that is not the main reason they laugh, _____ what we think.

6. Who laughs more in conversation, the speaker or the listener? Most people would guess the listener, but it is _____ the speaker.

7. Laughter has a _____ purpose: to help people live and work well together.

8. Provine describes laughter as "the oil in the social machine." Because his meaning may not be clear to the reader, the writer explains: "_____, it helps relationships between people work smoothly."

> **Vocabulary Tip:**
> *Actually* often introduces new information that may surprise the reader because it contrasts with what came before or with what the reader expects.

9. Jaak Panksepp does his research on laughter in a _____, or laboratory.

10. Panksepp said to be careful about tickling rats. He _____ people not to do it except in certain cases.

B. These sentences use the target words and phrases **in new contexts**. Complete them with the words and phrases in the box.

actually	expresses	in spite of	laughter	social
behavior	in other words	lab	prefer	warns

1. During the party, the room was full of the sounds of music, conversation, and _____.

2. Neighbors called the boy's parents to complain about his bad _____.

3. The sign _____ drivers that the road is bad and they should be careful.

4. The things you do with other people, especially for fun, make up your _____ life.

5. What would you _____ to do, go to a movie or go out to eat?

6. She claimed to be twenty-one, but she was _____ nineteen.

7. He almost never _____ his feelings or talks about anything personal.

8. The doctor had to wait for the results of the patient's medical tests to come back from the _____.

9. I usually stay inside when it rains, but today I went out for a walk _____ the rain.

> **Vocabulary Tip:**
> *Express* can take a reflexive pronoun as direct object (*myself, yourself,* etc.) or a noun: *express an opinion (an interest, your thanks, a hope).*

10. This street is a dead end. _____, it doesn't connect with another street, so you can't drive through.

C. Read the sentences. Guess the meaning of the **boldfaced** target words and phrases from the context. Match them with their definitions.

a. The children's mother warned them not to speak to **strangers**.

b. The scientists were interested in the effects of sleep on memory, so they did a **study**.

c. Do the police know who **carried out** the attack?

d. Joe traveled for twenty hours and changed planes three times, but the trip went **smoothly**.

e. Most magazines have photos of **attractive** people.

Target Word or Phrase	Definition
1. _____	= nice or pleasing to look at; interesting
2. _____	= happening without problems
3. _____	= people you do not know
4. _____	= did something that needed to be organized and planned
5. _____	= a piece of research done to find out more about a subject or problem

Building on the Vocabulary

Collocations: Verbs + Prepositions

Some verbs are often followed by a certain preposition. When a verb can take more than one preposition, its meaning may change. Check your dictionary for more information.

Here are some examples of verb + preposition pairs:

apply + to/for	*focus + on*
belong + to	*search + for*
compete + with/for	*train + for*
depend + on	*worry + about*

Complete the sentences. Add the preposition that goes with the verb.

1. These tools belong _____ my neighbor.

2. I depend _____ my friends for advice.

3. The runners are training _____ a big race.

4. I worried _____ the interview, but it went well.

5. Are you going to apply _____ the job?

6. He thinks the rules don't apply _____ him!

7. I speak slowly when I have to search _____ the right words.

8. The small bookstores can't compete _____ the big ones.

9. Stores compete _____ customers.

10. Music helps me focus _____ my homework.

DEVELOPING YOUR READING SKILLS

Clues to Meaning

> ### *In Other Words* and *That Is*
>
> Writers use a variety of ways to help the reader understand difficult parts of a text. Watch for the phrases *in other words* and *that is*. They often introduce an explanation of something the writer has just said.
>
> - *In other words* usually introduces a new sentence that repeats an idea but in a way that is easier to understand.
>   *Bees do a dance that describes both the direction and the distance to a food source. **In other words,** the dance tells other bees which way to go so they can fly straight to the food, and it tells them exactly how far to go.*
>
> - *That is* can also introduce a new sentence, or it can introduce just a word or phrase. The new information can be an explanation, a definition, or a synonym.
>   *The usual sleep schedule—**that is**, doing all your sleeping at night—might not be right for you.*

Look at "When and Why We Laugh." Find the definitions or explanations given for the **boldfaced** phrases below and copy them here.

1. "People have many ways to **express themselves**—_____
   _____ "

2. "Provine calls laughter '**the oil in the social machine**.' _____
   _____ "

Main Ideas

A. Which sentence gives the main idea of the reading? Check ☑ your answer.

- ☐ 1. Laughter is one type of human communication.
- ☐ 2. People laugh for many reasons but especially to connect with other people.
- ☐ 3. Certain animals use laughter in some of the same ways that human beings do.

> **Reading Tip:** The first paragraph of a text usually gives an introduction to the topic. The main idea of the text may be found there, often in the first or last sentence.

B. Write a sentence that gives the main idea of paragraph 4. If you use a part of the paragraph in your sentence, copy it exactly and put quotation marks before and after those words.

_____

_____

> **Writing Tip:** When you state the main idea of a text, make sure your statement is not too general or too specific.

Reading for Details

Read these questions about "When and Why We Laugh." Refer back to the reading and write short answers or complete sentences.

1. What two reasons for laughter do you find in the introduction?

   a. _____

   b. _____

2. Who did the study on laughter described in the reading? _____

3. Who was in the study?_____

   _____

4. What did the students have to do? _____

   _____

5. What did changes in the students' laughter depend on? _____

   _____

6. When did the female students in the study laugh most? _____

   _____

7. When did the male students laugh most? _____

   _____

8. In the second study, what effect did "high songlike laughs" have on listeners?

   _____

> **Reading Tip:** When a text describes a scientific study, read to find out who did the study, what they wanted to learn from it, how they did it, and what they found.

CRITICAL THINKING

Discussion

Talk about these questions in a small group.

1. How did the researchers carry out the first study described in the reading? Tell who took part in the study and what they had to do. What did the researchers find was true for *both* the men and the women? Would you volunteer for a study like this? Explain why or why not.

2. According to the reading, the female college students in the study

   a. laughed most with male friends

   b. laughed in a higher voice with male strangers

   Why do you think they laughed like this?

3. In the reading, Robert Provine says that laughter is "the oil in the social machine." What does that mean? How does it explain the finding that in conversation, the speaker laughs more than the listener? Explain your answer with examples from your own experience.

4. Find out the difference between *laughing with* someone and *laughing at* someone. Which kind of laughter are the researchers talking about in paragraph 4? Do the two kinds of laughter have the same social purpose? Explain your answer.

5. Research on laughter shows that the average adult laughs about seventeen times a day. Children laugh almost twice as often. How many times do you think you laugh during the day? What kinds of things make you laugh? Do you always laugh out loud, or do you sometimes laugh only to yourself?

WRITING

A. Use the Target Vocabulary: Choose five target words or phrases from the list on page 204. On a piece of paper, use each word or phrase in a sentence. Underline the target vocabulary. Then find a partner and read each other's sentences.

B. Practice Writing: Choose one of these topics and write a paragraph about it. Then find a partner and read each other's paragraphs.

1. Some people say, "Laughter is the best medicine." Do you agree? Why or why not?

2. "Laugh and the world laughs with you" is a common saying in English. Think of a common saying about laughter in another language you know. Tell what it is, what it means, and why you do or don't agree with it.

CHAPTER 19

The Inventor of the Telephone

The inventor of the telephone

LEARNING OUTCOME

❯ Learn about the man who invented the telephone

GETTING READY TO READ

Answer the questions below. Then discuss your answers in a small group.

1. Who invented the telephone?

☐ Thomas Edison   ☐ Guglielmo Marconi   ☐ Alexander Graham Bell

2. How many times a day do you usually use a phone to call someone?

☐ 0 to 2 times   ☐ 3 to 10 times   ☐ more than 10 times

3. How many times a day do you use a phone for some other reason?

☐ up to 10 times   ☐ 10 to 20 times   ☐ more than 20 times

Read to Find Out: What did people think about the telephone at first?

Look at the pictures, words, and definitions next to the reading. Then read without stopping.

The Inventor of the Telephone

1   If you cannot imagine how you would **get along without** your phone, then say a word of thanks to its inventor, Alexander Graham Bell. Bell was born in Scotland in 1847. All through his life, he had a strong interest in communication, **partly** because of his family. His grandfather was an actor and a famous **speech** teacher, and his father developed the first international phonetic alphabet.[1] His mother's influence was rather different. Communication was hard for her because she was almost completely **deaf**. She usually held a tube[2] to her ear **in order to** hear people. Her son Alexander discovered another way to communicate with her when he was a little boy. He used to **press** his mouth against her forehead[3] and speak in a low voice. The sound waves traveled to her ears through the bones of her head. This was among the first of his many discoveries about sound.

2   As a teenager, Bell taught music and public speaking at a boys' school. In his free time, he had fun working on **various** inventions with an older brother, inventions that included a useful machine for farmwork. Then both of Bell's brothers got sick and died. He **came down with** the same terrible sickness—tuberculosis[4]—leading his parents to move the family to Canada. There his health returned.

3   Bell moved to the United States when he was twenty-four. He went to Boston to teach at a school for deaf children. In Boston, he fell in love with Mabel Hubbard, a student of his who later became his wife. During this period of his life, Bell was a very busy man. **In addition to** teaching, he was working on several inventions.

4   Bell's main goal was to make machines to help deaf people hear. He was also trying to improve on[5] the telegraph.[6] In those days, the telegraph was the only way to send information quickly over a long distance. Telegraph messages traveled over **wires** and were sent in Morse code,[7] which used long and short sounds for the letters of the alphabet. Bell was trying to find a way to send the human voice along a wire. However, almost no one believed in this idea. People kept telling him, "You're **wasting** your time. You should try to invent a better telegraph—that's where the money is."

5   Bell understood a great deal about sound and electricity, but he was actually not very good at building things. Luckily, he met someone

[1] *phonetic alphabet* = a way to show the sounds of words, for example *laugh* = /læf/ or /läf/

[2] *a hearing tube*

[3] *forehead*

[4] *tuberculosis* = a serious sickness that affects a person's ability to breathe

[5] *improve on* = make something better than

[6] *a telegraph operator sending a message*

· · · — — — · · ·

[7] *Morse code for SOS, a call for help*

who was, a man named Thomas Watson. Watson turned out to be a great help to Bell. One day—it was March 10, 1876—the two men were working in **separate** rooms. They were getting ready to test a new invention, which had a wire going from one of the rooms to the other. Something **went wrong**, and Bell **shouted**, "Mr. Watson, come here. I want you!" His voice traveled along the wire, and Watson heard it coming from the new machine. It was the world's first telephone call. Bell may or may not have realized it at the time, but he was on his way to becoming a very rich man.

6 Soon **afterward**, Bell wrote to his father:

> The day is coming when telegraph wires will [go] to houses just like water or gas—and friends will converse with each other without leaving home.

Maybe his father laughed to hear this idea. At the time, most people expected the phone to be just a business tool, not something that anyone would ever have at home. Bell could see a greater future for it, but even he could probably never have imagined what phones are like today.

The quotation from Alexander Graham Bell's letter to his father comes from the April 1999 Library of Congress Information Bulletin. Retrieved February 11, 2016, from http://www.loc.gov/loc/lcib/9904/bell.html.

Quick Comprehension Check

A. Read these sentences. Circle T (true) or F (false). On the line, write the number of the paragraph with the answer.

1. Alexander Graham Bell's family influenced his career.   T   F   _____

2. Bell started inventing things while he was growing up.   T   F   _____

3. He was born and grew up in the United States.   T   F   _____

4. He never married.   T   F   _____

5. He invented the telephone working all alone.   T   F   _____

6. He believed that in the future, people would have phones at home.   T   F   _____

B. Work with your class. Share your answers from part A. Go back to the reading to find the reason why a statement is true or false. Correct the false statements.

EXPLORING VOCABULARY

Thinking about the Target Vocabulary

A. Look at the chart with the target vocabulary. Two nouns, five verbs, and three adjectives are missing. Scan the reading to find them, and add them to the correct places in the chart. Write the singular form of any plural noun. Write the base form of each verb.

¶	Nouns	Verbs	Adjectives	Other
1				
				partly
				in order to
2				
3				in addition to
4				
5				
				go wrong
6				afterward

B. Which target words or phrases are new to you? Circle them in the chart. Then find them in the reading. Look at the context. Can you guess the meaning?

Using the Target Vocabulary

A. These sentences are **about the reading**. Complete them with the words and phrases in the box.

deaf	in addition to	partly	speech	waste
get along without	in order to	separate	various	went wrong

1. For many of us, it is hard to imagine being without a phone. You might think you would not deal with that situation very well. You might think you could not _____ one.

2. Part of Bell's interest in communication was because of his family. It was _____ because of their influence.

3. Bell's grandfather taught people to speak well. He was a _____ teacher.

4. Bell's mother could hear only a little. She was almost completely _____.

> **Vocabulary Tip:**
> *Get along without someone/something* means to manage a situation or succeed without that person or thing. *Get along with someone* means to have a friendly relationship with them.

5. Bell's mother used a hearing tube _____ hear what people around her were saying. The tube made sounds louder.

6. As a teenager, Bell and his brother built a variety of things together. They worked on _____ inventions.

7. Bell had a teaching job in Boston. He also had more to do. _____ his job, he worked on several inventions.

> **Writing Tip:** You can use *in addition* without *to*: Bell taught deaf students. In addition, he worked on inventions.

8. People told Bell to use his time carefully. They told him not to _____ his time.

9. On March 10, 1876, Bell and his partner were not working in the same room. They were in _____ rooms.

10. While he was working, Bell had an accident of some kind. Something _____.

B. These sentences use the target words and phrases **in new contexts**. Complete them with the words and phrases in the box.

deaf	go wrong	in order to	separate	various
get along without	in addition to	partly	speech	waste

1. The sky was only _____ cloudy in the morning, but completely cloudy later on.

2. You'll have to speak in a loud voice in order for him to hear you. He's getting _____.

> **Vocabulary Tip:** The adjective *various* is related to the noun *variety* and the verb *vary*.

3. The first cars were all black. Now cars are available in _____ colors.

4. Only human beings can express themselves through _____.

5. People use laughter and other sounds to communicate _____ using words.

6. You don't need a car in this city. You can _____ one very well using buses and the subway.

7. Relax! I'm sure everything will go smoothly. Nothing will _____.

8. We saw that movie, and it was very disappointing. Don't _____ your money on it.

9. He took science courses _____ prepare for a career in medicine.

> **Vocabulary Tip:** *Separate* can be an adjective, a noun, or a verb, but the pronunciation of the verb is a little different.

10. The student kept her notes for each of her courses in _____ parts of her notebook.

C. Read each definition and look at the paragraph number. Look back at the reading on pages 212–213 to find the **boldfaced** word or phrase to match the definition. Copy it in the chart.

Vocabulary Tip:
Afterward (or *afterwards*) means "after (an event already mentioned):" *We had dinner, and afterward, we watched a movie.*

Definition	Paragraph	Target Word or Phrase
1. push something against something else	1	
2. started to have (a sickness)	2	
3. long, thin pieces of metal, like threads, used for carrying electricity or sound **waves**	4	
4. said something in a very loud voice	5	
5. after that	6	

Building on the Vocabulary

Word Grammar: Nouns as Modifiers

Nouns can modify other nouns. That is, they can act like adjectives, as in:

The **sound waves** traveled to her ears.

It was the world's first **telephone call**.

Most people expected the phone to be just a **business tool**.

Underline the seven nouns that modify other nouns.

1. The boys are working on their science projects.
2. I planted some flower seeds in my vegetable garden.
3. Did you check the bus schedule?
4. Gail showed her communication skills at her job interview.
5. Doctors sometimes wear white lab coats.

DEVELOPING YOUR READING SKILLS

Text Organization

Look back at "The Inventor of the Telephone." How is the information in the reading organized? Check ☑ your answer.

☐ 1. Each paragraph compares one thing with another.

☐ 2. Each paragraph describes a cause and effect relationship.

☐ 3. The paragraphs are in chronological order (time order).

Critical Thinking Tip: Notice the way the writer has organized the information in a text. That will help you focus on the key ideas and relationships and understand what to expect next as you read.

Making Inferences

Are the following statements true or false? You cannot scan the reading for the answers. You must infer them. Circle T or F, and give one or more reasons for your answer.

1. Alexander Graham Bell was probably close to his family.　　　Ⓣ　　F

   His family influenced his career, and he and his brother invented

   things together.

2. Tuberculosis was a more serious sickness in the 1800s than it is now.　　　T　　F

   _____

   _____

3. Bell's wife was deaf.　　　T　　F

   _____

   _____

4. What Bell wanted most in life was to become rich and famous.　　　T　　F

   _____

   _____

5. Thomas Watson believed in Bell's ideas when others did not.　　　T　　F

   _____

   _____

Summarizing

On a piece of paper, write a summary of "The Inventor of the Telephone." Use no more than ten sentences. Use your own words. That is, do not copy sentences from the reading. Include:

- the inventor's name
- why he is famous
- when and where he was born
- where he spent most of his life
- his main goal as an inventor
- the date of the first phone call

CRITICAL THINKING

Discussion

Talk about these questions in a small group.

1. The reading says that Alexander Graham Bell began teaching at a young age. How do you think his father, grandfather, and mother influenced his choice of career? Today, do you think families play as big a part in the career choices that young people make? Explain your answer.

2. How old do you think Bell was when he and his family left Scotland for Canada? What information in the reading supports your answer? What made the family leave? Today, is this still a reason why people leave their countries?

3. Would you agree that most inventions are the result of a lot of work? Do you think that that was true of the first telephone? To do something that takes a lot of work, people usually need to feel motivated—that is, something drives them to work long and hard to reach a goal. What do you think motivated Bell? Underline the parts of the reading that support your answer.

4. True or False: People gave Bell a lot of support for his efforts to send a human voice over a wire. Explain your answer. How do you think people's advice affected Bell?

5. The word *visionary* means someone who has clear ideas and strong feelings about the way something should be, or could be, in the future. The word is often used for people who are able to imagine the future in a way that others cannot. What famous people do you think of as visionaries? (It could be a political or religious leader, an artist or writer, or another inventor.) Would you call Alexander Graham Bell a visionary? Explain.

WRITING

A. Use the Target Vocabulary: Choose five target words or phrases from the list on page 214. On a piece of paper, use each word or phrase in a sentence. Underline the target vocabulary. Then find a partner and read each other's sentences.

B. Practice Writing: Choose one of these topics and write a paragraph about it. Then find a partner and read each other's paragraphs.

1. How important are phones in your life? Write about your relationship with the telephone.

2. Use your imagination to complete this sentence: *I wish somebody would invent* . . . . Explain why this invention would be a good thing.

> **Writing Tip:** Your phone may play many roles in your life. Before you start your paragraph, try drawing a concept map of all these roles.

CHAPTER 20

Speaking with Your Eyes

LEARNING OUTCOME

❯ Learn about how people communicate with their eyes

Making eye contact

GETTING READY TO READ

Talk about these questions with your class.

1. Do you know the phrase *nonverbal communication*? It refers to communication that happens without words. Give examples of how you can say something:

   by using your face

   by using your hands

   by moving or standing

2. How can you read people by looking at their nonverbal communication? That is, how do you understand what they are communicating?

3. Do you think people are usually aware of the messages they send nonverbally, or are they communicating without realizing it? Give examples to support your answer.

Read to Find Out: What influences our eye behavior?

Look at the picture, words, and definitions next to the reading. Then read without stopping.

Speaking with Your Eyes

1   When we think about communicating with other people, we usually think about talking or writing. That is, we think about using words. However, much of the communication that takes place **in person** happens without words. It happens through nonverbal communication. We send nonverbal messages in many ways, **including** with our face, our hands, and the way we stand, move, and use the **space** around us. We get messages from others in the same way. Our eyes play an especially important role. Researchers who study this role use the **term** *eye behavior*. It **refers to** both the things we do with our eyes without realizing it and the things we do **on purpose**.

2   One area of eye behavior is eye contact.[1] Imagine yourself walking along a busy city sidewalk.[2] What are your eyes doing? Do you focus on anything, or are your eyes moving all the time? What are other people's eyes doing? If you are in a U.S. city, there are probably few people making eye contact. If your eyes meet a stranger's, **chances are** that he or she will quickly look away. If the stranger does not look away but **maintains** eye contact, it may be a **sign** of **attraction**.

3   Eye contact shows that we are paying attention. It may mean nothing more than we are being **polite**. Or it may mean something else. We often use our eyes to express interest in someone. Because it is natural to look at things we find attractive, keeping our eyes on someone can be like paying the person a compliment.[3]

4   Looking at something attractive actually **brings about** a change in our eyes. It makes our pupils—those small **round** black areas in the middle of our eyes—grow larger. Large pupils then make our eyes more attractive.

5   Research has shown that eye contact can also influence whether someone finds another person attractive. In a study at the University of Aberdeen in Scotland, Dr. Claire Conway asked participants[4] to look at photos of faces. There were photos of people smiling and looking **directly** at the viewer,[5] and there were photos of those same people smiling but looking away. Dr. Conway said, "Faces that were looking directly at the viewer were considered more attractive." This was especially true for faces of the opposite sex. Dr. Conway suggests that something in the human brain makes us prefer the faces of people who

[1] *eye contact =
two people
looking at each
other's eyes at
the same time*

[2] *a sidewalk*

[3] *pay someone a
compliment =
tell someone
something nice
about
themselves*

[4] *participant =
someone who
is taking part
in an activity or
event*

[5] *viewer = a
person who
is looking or
watching*

make eye contact with us. When they are looking at us, they seem to like us. If they like us, that makes them more attractive to us.

6   Of course, a face in a photo is one thing, and a real person looking at you is something else. How do you feel when someone makes eye contact with you and keeps on looking? Does it make the person seem attractive, or does it make you feel uncomfortable, or even afraid?

7   How we read people's eye behavior depends in part on our culture. In some cultures, making and keeping eye contact is a sign of respect. In others, it has the opposite effect. As we grow up, we learn the rules of our culture for nonverbal communication in general and eye contact in particular.[6] We learn what we are expected to do and what we are **allowed** to do. But even as an adult, you may find there is still more to learn about the language of the eyes.

[6] *in particular =* especially

Quick Comprehension Check

A. Read these sentences. Circle T (true) or F (false). On the line, write the number of the paragraph with the answer.

1. We use our eyes in nonverbal communication.   T   F   _____

2. Eye behavior is the same across cultures.   T   F   _____

3. Making eye contact means looking at someone   T   F   _____
    else's eyes.

4. We might or might not realize what we are doing   T   F   _____
    with our eyes.

5. Eye contact can mean "I like you."   T   F   _____

6. We are attracted to people who seem to like us.   T   F   _____

B. Work with your class. Share your answers from part A. Go back to the reading to find the reason why a sentence is true or false. Correct the false sentences.

EXPLORING VOCABULARY

Thinking about the Target Vocabulary

A. Look at the chart with the target vocabulary. Four nouns, four verbs, and two adjectives are missing. Scan the reading to find them, and add them to the correct places in the chart. Write the base form of each verb.

¶	Nouns	Verbs	Adjectives	Other
1				in person
				including
				on purpose
2				chances are
3				
4				
5				directly
7				

B. Which target words or phrases are new to you? Circle them in the chart. Then find them in the reading. Look at the context. Can you guess the meaning?

Using the Target Vocabulary

A. These sentences are **about the reading**. What is the meaning of each **boldfaced** word or phrase? Circle a, b, or c.

1. You can talk to someone either **in person**, on the phone, or by computer. *In person* means

   a. in someone's ear.
   b. in the same place with someone.
   c. by shouting at someone.

2. The **term** *eye behavior* refers to what our eyes do. A term is

   a. a word or phrase.
   b. a study.
   c. an explanation.

3. Use *eye behavior* to **refer to** both the things we do with our eyes knowingly and the things we do without realizing it. *Refer to* means

   a. claim.
   b. search.
   c. mean.

   > **Vocabulary Tip:**
   > *Refer to* has several meanings and uses. Look it up in your dictionary to learn more.

4. When you choose to look at someone, you look at them **on purpose**. *On purpose* means

   a. by accident.
   b. in a planned way.
   c. partly.

5. Sometimes people make eye contact and **maintain** it. *Maintain something* means

   a. make it continue.
   b. get along without it.
   c. prefer it.

6. Looking someone in the eye (that is, making eye contact) can show **attraction**. *Attraction* means

   a. a readiness to fight.
   b. a sense of being bored.
   c. a strong feeling of liking.

7. Looking at something or someone you like **brings about** a change in your eyes. *Bring something about* means

   a. notice it.
   b. figure it out.
   c. cause it to happen.

8. The pupils of your eyes are **round**. *Round* means

   a. calm and relaxed.
   b. strong and secure.
   c. shaped like a circle or a ball.

9. People in the study preferred faces that were looking **directly** at them. *Directly* means

   a. nearly.
   b. straight.
   c. unfortunately.

10. Cultural rules tell us what we can do and what we are not **allowed** to do. If you allow people to do something, you

    a. realize that they are doing it.
    b. explain how to do it.
    c. let them do it.

B. These sentences use the target words and phrases **in new contexts**. Complete them with the words and phrases in the box.

allowed	bring about	in person	on purpose	round
attraction	directly	maintaining	refer to	terms

1. The owner of the café set some small _____ tables out on the sidewalk and placed chairs around them.

2. In the game of soccer, only the goalkeeper is _____ to touch the ball with his or her hands.

3. People use *profession* to _____ certain types of jobs only, jobs for which you need a lot of education or advanced training.

4. The boy felt bad about breaking his little sister's toy. He didn't do it _____.

5. The bank is _____ across the street from the post office.

6. I didn't understand some of the _____ the professor used in her lecture.

7. You can apply for the job online, or you can go to the company and apply _____.

8. The company works hard at _____ good relationships with its customers.

9. The greatest leaders _____ the most important political changes.

10. The man was so boring that Carol's friends couldn't understand her _____ to him.

C. Read the sentences. Guess the meaning of the **boldfaced** target words and phrases from the context. Match them with their definitions.

a. Those birds are a **sign** that winter is ending and spring is coming.

b. Jack hates riding on crowded trains. He needs a lot of personal **space**.

c. It's **polite** to say *Please* and *Thank you*.

d. There were eight people at John's birthday dinner, **including** John and his wife.

e. If you review your notes for the test, **chances are** you'll do well on it.

> **Vocabulary Tip:**
> *Sign* can be a noun or a verb. It has many meanings and uses. See your dictionary to learn more.

Target Word or Phrase		Definition
1. _____	=	the empty area between people or things
2. _____	=	an event or fact that shows that something is happening
3. _____	=	it is probably true that
4. _____	=	having something as a part (of a larger group)
5. _____	=	behaving or speaking correctly for the social situation you are in, considering other people's needs and feelings

Building on the Vocabulary

Word Grammar: *Allow* vs. *Let*

The verbs *allow* and *let* have the same meaning, but they are used differently in sentences.

allow:
- Use *allow* + someone + *to* + verb: *Please allow my son to leave school at 1:30 today.*
- Use *be* + *allowed to* + verb: *You aren't allowed to park there.*
- Use *allow* + noun (or verb + *-ing*): *Do they allow pets? Do they allow smoking?*

let:
- Use *let* + someone + verb: *Please let my son leave school at 1:30 today.*

Complete the sentences. Use *allow* or *let*.

1. My parents wouldn't _____ me have a dog.

2. The high school doesn't _____ students to park in that lot.

3. _____ the other car go first.

4. Will the teacher _____ dictionaries during the test?

5. The town does not _____ fishing at the public beach.

DEVELOPING YOUR READING SKILLS

Definitions

Defining Terms

Sometimes a writer defines a word in the text. Sometimes readers must define terms for themselves, based on information in the text. When you see a term used repeatedly in a text, be sure that you understand it well. Test your understanding by trying to define the term.

If a word you want to define is a verb, you might be able to use this pattern:

(verb)

When you _____, you _____

*When you **allow** something, you let it happen.*

For any part of speech, you can use this pattern:

(word or phrase)

" _____ " means _____

"Pay someone a compliment" means tell the person something nice about themselves.

Use information from the reading to write definitions of these terms.

1. make eye contact _____

   _____

   _____

2. nonverbal communication _____

   _____

   _____

3. eye behavior _____

   _____

   _____

Understanding Cause and Effect

Use information from the reading to complete the diagram.

Cause		Effect
1.	→	the pupils of your eyes grow larger
2. large pupils	→	
3. a face in a photo is smiling and looking directly at you	→	
4. someone makes and maintains eye contact	→	Depending on the culture, it shows: (a) (b)

Fact vs. Opinion

A. Decide if each statement expresses a fact or an opinion. Base your answers on information from the reading. Circle Fact or Opinion.

1. Eye behavior is a form of nonverbal communication.   Fact / Opinion
2. Making eye contact is one type of eye behavior.   Fact / Opinion
3. People naturally look at things they find attractive.   Fact / Opinion
4. It is a bad idea to make eye contact with strangers.   Fact / Opinion
5. Your culture influences your eye behavior.   Fact / Opinion
6. You should look people in the eye to show respect.   Fact / Opinion

B. Write two sentences.

1. Write a fact about eye behavior. Use information from the reading.

_____

_____

_____

2. Write an opinion of your own about eye behavior.

_____

_____

_____

CRITICAL THINKING

Discussion

Talk about these questions in a small group.

1. According to the reading, what eye behavior would you expect of people walking along a busy city sidewalk in the United States? Would it be the same or different on a street in your hometown? Explain.

2. Look again at paragraph 3. What does "It" mean in this sentence: "It may mean nothing more than we are being polite"? What does "nothing more than" mean? The paragraph goes on to say, "Or it may mean something else." What else could it mean?

3. Read paragraph 6 again. The writer asks several questions. How would you answer them? How would your answers vary in different situations? Do your answers agree with the findings of Dr. Conway's study of eye contact? Explain.

4. Read the last paragraph again. What is the main idea? In your culture, how do people use eye behavior to show respect?

5. When people wear sunglasses, we cannot see their eyes. What effect do you think wearing sunglasses has on a person's eye behavior? What effect might their sunglasses have on other people? Why?

> **Critical Thinking:** Question 2 is about pronoun reference. Make sure you know who or what each pronoun in a text refers to. Be aware that words like *this, one,* and *another* can function as pronouns.

> **Reading Tip:** The main idea of a text is often introduced in the first paragraph and restated in the last paragraph. It may help you better understand the main idea of a text if you reread the beginning and the end.

WRITING

A. Use the Target Vocabulary: Choose five target words or phrases from the list on page 223. On a piece of paper, use each word or phrase in a sentence. Underline the target vocabulary. Then find a partner and read each other's sentences.

B. Practice Writing: Choose one of these topics and write a paragraph about it. Then find a partner and read each other's paragraphs.

1. When is it important to make eye contact? Give some advice for making eye contact and using other kinds of nonverbal communication to a person who is going to visit your country.

2. There are many well-known sayings about eyes in English, such as "The eyes are the window to the soul," meaning that you can understand what is in a person's mind and heart by looking into their eyes. Give a saying about eyes from another language you know, explain what it means, and give your opinion about it.

> **Writing Tip:** If you quote a common saying, remember to put quotation marks before and after it.

Checkpoint

LOOK BACK

A. Think About This

Look back at your answers to the *Think About This* question on page 191:
What do people do to communicate?
Can you add anything?

B. Remember the Readings

What do you want to remember most from the readings in Unit 5?
For each chapter, write one sentence about the reading.

Chapter 17: Who Does It Better?

_____

Chapter 18: When and Why We Laugh

_____

Chapter 19: The Inventor of the Telephone

_____

Chapter 20: Speaking with Your Eyes

_____

REVIEWING VOCABULARY

A. Match the words in the box with their definitions. There are four extra words.

actually	deaf	lab	prefer	speech	voice
allow	invention	male	sense	stranger	warn

1. _____ = unable to hear

2. _____ = really and truly (even though it may surprise you)

3. _____ = the ability to speak, or the spoken language

4. _____ = the sound someone makes when singing or speaking

5. _____ = know or feel something without seeing it or being told about it

6. _____ = like or want (some person or thing) more than another

7. _____ = someone that you do not know

8. _____ = tell someone that something bad or dangerous may happen

B. Complete the sentences with words or phrases from the box. There are two extra words or phrases.

bring about	coming down with	in addition to	in spite of
carrying out	get along	in order to	including
chances are	go wrong	in person	on purpose

1. I don't feel well. I think I'm _____ a cold.

2. It took years of effort to _____ a change in the law.

3. If you try to call her before 10:00 A.M., _____ she'll still be asleep.

4. I had to take two buses _____ get there.

5. Somehow he manages to do a weekend job _____ his regular job.

6. He claims it was an accident, but I think he did it _____.

7. I really need my car. I couldn't _____ without it.

8. The bill comes to $19.95, _____ the tax.

9. You can apply by mail, but it's faster to do it _____.

10. Have you thought about what to do if things _____?

EXPANDING VOCABULARY

Complete the chart of word families with **boldfaced** words from the sentences below.

	Nouns	Verbs	Adjectives	Adverbs
1.	attraction	attract	attractive	attractively
2.				
3.				
4.				
5.				

1. a. Flowers **attract** certain insects, like bees.
   b. She is an **attractive** young woman.
   c. She is always **attractively** dressed.
   d. It was easy to see the **attraction** between Jack and Diana.
2. a. It was just a friendly **competition**.
   b. Their products are **competitively** priced.
   c. He and his brother are highly **competitive**.
   d. I give up! I can't **compete** with you.
3. a. That actor has very **expressive** eyes.
   b. Did you see the **expression** on her face when she got the news?
   c. It's hard for me to **express** myself.
   d. He sings so **expressively**!
4. a. Do boys and girls go to **separate** schools in your country?
   b. They arrived at the party **separately** but left together.
   c. **Separate** the light-colored clothes from the dark ones before washing them.
   d. They were married for five years before their **separation**.
5. a. Don't **waste** water.
   b. Taxpayers get angry if the government spends **wastefully**.
   c. What a **waste** of time!
   d. He'll have to change his **wasteful** spending habits.

A PUZZLE

Complete the sentences with words you studied in Chapters 17–20. Write the words in the puzzle.

ACROSS

2. Before you leave the plane, check for your

   _____ belongings. Make sure you have everything that belongs to you.

3. The shortest distance between two points

   is a _____ line.

6. It was a great game. _____, we went out to celebrate the win.

8. My mother said, "Don't stare at people. It's

   not _____."

10. Al got the job _____ his own efforts, not because of family connections.

11. The sound of _____ filled the room.

DOWN

1. Pam's strange _____ worried her friends—things like suddenly laughing for no reason.

3. Joe has many friends and a busy

   _____ life.

4. The letter "O" is _____ in shape.

5. His socks are all black or white, but I have

   socks in _____ colors.

7. You'll have two weeks of

   _____ when you start the job.

9. The _____ was wet and muddy after the rain.

BUILDING DICTIONARY SKILLS

A. Words often have more than one meaning. Look at this entry for *direction*. Write the number of the meaning used in each sentence below.

_____ 1. Read the **directions** before you start the test.

_____ 2. *A one-way street* means traffic goes in one **direction** only.

_____ 3. His life is taking a new **direction**.

_____ 4. He has a good sense of **direction**, but he depends on his GPS when driving somewhere new.

_____ 5. The company has grown under McCrae's **direction**.

> **di•rec•tion** /dəˈrɛkʃən, daɪ-/ n.
>
> **1** [C] the way someone or something is moving, facing, or aimed: *Brian drove off **in the direction of** (=toward) the party.* | *As she walked along the trail, she saw a large man coming in **the opposite direction**.* **2** [C] the general way in which someone or something changes or develops: *Suddenly the conversation changed direction.* **3 directions** [plural] instructions about how to go from one place to another, or about how to do something: *Could you **give** me **directions to** the airport?* | *Read the directions at the top of the page.* **4** [U] control, guidance, or advice: *The company's been successful **under Martini's direction**.* **5** [U] a general purpose or aim: *Sometimes I feel that my life lacks direction.* **6 sense of direction** the ability to know which way to go in a place you do not know well.

B. Look at the entries for *sign*. Then look at the use of *sign* in each sentence below. Write the part of speech (POS) and the number of the meaning.

> **sign¹** /saɪn/ n. [C] **1** a piece of paper, metal, etc. with words or a picture that gives people information, a warning, or instructions: *Follow the signs for Exit 3A.* | *a no-smoking sign* **2** an event, fact, etc. that shows something is true, is happening, or will happen: *An invitation for a second job interview is a good sign.* | *warning signs of cancer* **3** a picture of shape that has a certain meaning SYN **symbol**: *A dollar sign looks like "$."* **4** a movement or sound you make without speaking, in order to tell someone something: *He gave me a thumbs-up sign.* | *sign language* **5** one of the symbols of the ZODIAC.
>
> **sign²** v. **1** [I,T] to write your name on a letter or document to show you wrote it or agree with it, or to make it official: *Please sign on this line.* | *Both countries signed the agreement.* **2** [T] to officially agree to employ someone: *The Barcelona team signed him to a three-year contract.*

POS	No.	
n.	4	1. The police officer raised a hand as a **sign** to cars to stop.
		2. We both **signed** the car rental agreement.
		3. A plus **sign** looks like "+."
		4. Stop **signs** in the United States are red.
		5. Does the rain show any **sign** of stopping?

Vocabulary Self-Test 3

Circle the letter of the word or phrase that best completes each sentence.

1. Long-_____ phone calls used to be very expensive.
   a. root   b. distance   c. laughter   d. score

2. Tim asked me for advice, and I _____ that he call you instead.
   a. competed   b. afforded   c. suggested   d. joined

3. The books were so _____ that it was clear no one had touched them in a long while.
   a. attractive   b. dusty   c. popular   d. female

4. There were no problems. Everything went _____.
   a. partly   b. rather   c. unfortunately   d. smoothly

5. Elizabeth kept her jacket on _____ the heat.
   a. forward   b. in order to   c. in spite of   d. nearly

6. Paul _____ that he can tell what I'm thinking by the look on my face.
   a. claims   b. wastes   c. melts   d. matters

7. I've seen him do some dangerous things. That man has no
   _____!
   a. basis   b. behavior   c. fear   d. oxygen

8. I saw only the front page of the newspaper, but Lora read the
   _____ thing.
   a. professional b. specific   c. low   d. entire

9. Of course she's upset. _____, you promised to help her, and now you say you can't.
   a. No longer   b. After all   c. No matter   d. Whenever

10. We'll have to finish talking about this later. The meeting _____ to start.

    a. is about   b. is offering   c. goes on   d. in addition

11. The more energy a sound _____ has, the louder the sound is.

    a. wire   b. amount   c. wave   d. weight

12. This weekend, we'll have to _____ our clocks back one hour.

    a. concern   b. set   c. share   d. attract

13. He's shorter _____ than he looks on TV.

    a. in person   b. right away   c. on purpose   d. except

14. Mary had to close down her business. I don't know what _____.

    a. went wrong   b. got along   c. figured out   d. made up

15. The researchers _____ a study on how chocolate affects the brain.

    a. turned into   b. came down with   c. sensed   d. carried out

16. Henry has never given a speech before. _____ he's nervous. Wouldn't you be?

    a. For one thing   b. No doubt   c. Immediately   d. Including

17. Dr. Hernandez has had a fifty-two-year _____ in medicine.

    a. purpose   b. shock   c. career   d. stranger

18. The cat lay very _____ while watching the bird.

    a. powerful   b. personal   c. round   d. still

19. The house is 200 _____ years old.

    a. or so   b. lab   c. male   d. daily

20. David _____ to leave work early without anyone in the office knowing.

    a. warned   b. managed   c. noticed   d. advanced

21. Did you _____ good eye contact during your interview?

    a. hide   b. express   c. support   d. maintain

22. The sick man didn't try to speak. It was too much of an _____.

    a. attraction   b. invitation   c. increase   d. effort

23. There was a foot of snow on the _____.

    a. study   b. ground   c. choice   d. period

24. Ann invented a new _____ for recycling plastic.

    a. space   b. term   c. system   d. variety

25. The boy doesn't mean to hurt other children, but he doesn't

    _____ how strong he is.

    a. realize   b. lead   c. prefer   d. develop

26. I thought her name was Joan, but it's _____ JoAnne.

    a. according to   b. however   c. naturally   d. actually

27. The woman in the photo seemed to be looking _____ at me.

    a. in general   b. directly   c. afterward   d. highly

28. We couldn't find two seats together on the train, so we sat in

    _____ places.

    a. social   b. secure   c. separate   d. brave

29. The company will offer more training at _____ times during the next year.

    a. straight   b. weak   c. sharp   d. various

30. Changes in class size will _____ all teachers and students.

    a. affect   b. take part   c. attack   d. escape

31. The tax increase will not _____ to anyone who makes less than $25,000 a year.

    a. apply   b. contain   c. review   d. feed

32. After a great deal of hard work, he _____ his goal.

    a. turned out   b. reached   c. prepared   d. rushed

33. You can _____ the results of your test tomorrow.

    a. disappear   b. encourage   c. expect   d. stare

34. Nancy never remembers her dreams, _____ her sister records hers in a notebook every morning.

    a. except   b. alike   c. through   d. while

35. _____ Dan has the right tools for the job, he really doesn't have the skills.

    a. Somehow   b. Chances are   c. Once   d. Although

36. We were glad to see _____ that Mom is finally feeling better.

    a. memories   b. directions   c. signs   d. speech

37. I _____ understood anything he said. What about you? Could you understand him at all?

    a. hardly   b. supply   c. politely   d. basically

38. The prison _____ visitors only on weekends.

    a. presses   b. allows   c. divides   d. creates

39. I can hear you perfectly well. You don't have to _____.

    a. deaf   b. shout   c. voice   d. pronounce

40. _____ that you review your notes for the next test.

    a. Get over   b. Bring about   c. Refer to   d. Make sure

See the Answer Key on page 239.

Vocabulary Self-Test Answer Key

Below are the answers to the Vocabulary Self-Tests. Check your answers, and then review any words you did not remember. You can look up a word in the Index to Target Vocabulary on pages 241–242. Then go back to the reading and exercises to find the word. Use your dictionary as needed.

Vocabulary Self-Test 1, Units 1 and 2 (pages 91–93)

1. d. gets to	11. b. figure out	21. d. power
2. a. choice	12. c. basis	22. a. hardly
3. a. no doubt	13. c. opposite	23. b. is about to
4. c. boring	14. a. mentioned	24. c. difference
5. d. reach	15. a. average	25. a. cover
6. b. hide	16. a. areas	26. b. nearly
7. a. specific	17. b. Although	27. c. aware
8. d. danger	18. d. deal with	28. d. available
9. b. weigh	19. c. control	29. take part
10. a. instead	20. b. talent	

Vocabulary Self-Test 2, Units 3 and 4 (pages 188–190)

1. b. amounts	11. d. situation	21. c. environment
2. c. search	12. b. certain	22. b. region
3. a. exactly	13. c. fair	23. c. gentle
4. d. That is	14. a. focus	24. c. closet
5. a. destroyed	15. c. rate	25. a. series
6. d. make up	16. a. no matter	26. b. mean
7. b. efforts	17. a. set	27. b. According to
8. c. record	18. b. emotions	28. d. up to
9. d. put up with	19. b. calm	29. c. notes
10. a. make a difference	20. a. supplies	

Vocabulary Self-Test 3, Units 1–5 (pages 235–238)

1. b. distance
2. c. suggested
3. b. dusty
4. d. smoothly
5. c. in spite of
6. a. claims
7. c. fear
8. d. entire
9. b. After all
10. a. is about
11. c. wave
12. b. set
13. a. in person
14. a. went wrong
15. d. carried out
16. b. No doubt
17. c. career
18. d. still
19. a. or so
20. b. managed
21. d. maintain
22. d. effort
23. b. ground
24. c. system
25. a. realize
26. d. actually
27. b. directly
28. c. separate
29. d. various
30. a. affect
31. a. apply
32. b. reached
33. c. expect
34. d. while
35. d. Although
36. c. signs
37. a. hardly
38. b. allows
39. b. shout
40. d. Make sure

Index to Target Vocabulary